Reel Conversations

Reel Conversations

Reading Films
with Young Adults

Alan B. Teasley & Ann Wilder

Heinemann
Boynton/Cook Publishers
Portsmouth, NH

Boynton/Cook Publishers
A subsidiary of Reed Elsevier Inc.
361 Hanover Street
Portsmouth, NH 03801-3912

Offices and agents throughout the world

Library of Congress Cataloging-in-Publication Data
Teasley, Alan B.
    Reel conversations: reading films with young adults/Alan B. Teasley & Ann Wilder.
        p.   cm.
    Includes filmographies and bibliographical references.
    ISBN 0-86709-377-3
    1. Motion pictures—Study and teaching. 2. Visual literacy. 3. Motion pictures in education. 4. English literature—Study and teaching. I. Wilder, Ann.   II. Title.
PN1993.7.T4 1996
791.43′071′2—dc20   96-30441
                                                         CIP

Editor: Peter S. Stillman
Consulting editor: Virginia Monseau
Cover design: Jenny Jensen Greenleaf
Manufacturing: Louise Richardson

Printed in the United States of America on acid-free paper.
99 98   DA   2 3 4 5 6

To our parents

Beth and Baxter Teasley
Sterly and Pelham Wilder

Contents

Part II
The Major Themes of Young Adult Films

A Letter to Our Readers

Dear Reader,

As we've written this book, we've had several audiences in mind—beginning and veteran teachers, teachers who've taught films frequently, and those who haven't started yet.

If you're a first-year teacher, if you've just not taught many films, or if you are simply at a loss as to what to do with a film, we recommend you read the first chapter and then try the activities in Chapter Two. If you've never taught film terminology before, give yourself some lead time. Notice film techniques in your own viewing. You don't have to be an expert. Remember that your chief task will be to facilitate the students' analysis of the clips. Embark on this as a mutual voyage of discovery. Once you've gained some confidence with the skills of "reading a movie," you'll be ready to move on to a more in-depth study of individual films with the activities in Chapter Three.

If you are a veteran teacher who has used film frequently in the classroom, we hope that Chapters One and Three will provide you with affirmation for your current strategies. If you've already been teaching visual analysis of film and are looking for additional ideas, you might want to start with the viewer-response strategies of Chapter Three or explore teaching film genres as described in Chapter Four. Chapter Five contains ideas for integrating film with the study of literature as well as for teaching elective courses in mass media and film.

In our workshops, teachers often ask: Since I haven't done much with film yet, does it take a lot of time to get started? We hope that we've given you enough ideas and strategies that you could use at least some of the recommended lessons without a lot of preparation. Of course, you will have to watch the films in advance and plan for the discussion breaks. Over the years, we have invested hours planning film units, but the majority of that time was spent watching a number of films to find one that would work with our students. We hope that our numerous annotated lists of films will save you time you would have otherwise spent previewing films.

Before you dive in, we want to explain how we have cited films and how we have noted the timing of film clips. In the absence of a universally recognized standard for film citations, we have chosen to provide the information that (1) will help you locate the film and (2) will give you crucial information you need to plan your lessons. We've found that we can access most films by just their title. In the case of multiple films with the same title (for example, the three instances of *Stagecoach* and more of *Hamlet)*, the year of release or the director's name usually serves to distinguish one film from another. We expect you'll want to know the rating of each film for planning purposes, so we have included the Motion Picture Association of America (MPAA) rating and noted nonrated films as "NR," a designation that may mean that the film was made before the rating system was implemented (1968) or that it was never submitted for rating (as is the case with many foreign films). We've included the running time (in minutes) as reported in reference sources or on the video box. For the data in the citations, we have relied on *VideoHound's Golden Movie Retriever* (Detroit: Visible Ink Press, 1995).

When we have referred to a specific clip from a film, we have designated it by starting and ending times (in the form [hour:minute:second]) as timed from the beginning of the film. Since videotapes may contain previews, ads, and an irregular length of blank tape, we have timed the clips from the studio logo or just after the FBI warning, whichever is closest to the actual start of the film. Please consider the timings approximate and always adjust the clip to your instructional purpose.

Finally, we hope that you will honor the spirit in which we offer these strategies. There is some serious fun to be had here. Whatever you do, keep the study of film lively and engaging.

Sincerely,
Alan Teasley
Ann Wilder

Acknowledgments

This book would not have been possible without the support, suggestions, and encouragement of our friends and colleagues both in our local community of teachers and in the National Council of Teachers of English (NCTE).

We take this opportunity to express our thanks and sincere appreciation:

To Ann's students—at Chewning Middle School, Duke Young Writers' Camp, and Southern High School—who over the past decade have been generous in sharing their insights about film.

To Alan's students in Duke University's undergraduate and graduate programs in English education for providing feedback about teaching strategies and for trying out the strategies during their student teaching.

To Ann's colleagues in the English Department at Southern High School, particularly Debbie Andrews, Becky Marsten, Michelle Lyn, and Meggan Piehl, who have used our ideas and shared theirs with us over the past ten years.

To Van Garrison, who was with us at our first conference presentation, who invited Alan to bring *Citizen Kane* to her American Lit and advanced placement (AP) classes, and who continues to collaborate with us.

To Dr. Ron Gilliard, former principal of Southern High School, for trusting Ann's judgment in teaching film and for supporting her attendance at NCTE conferences for the last eight years.

To Nancy Duffner, Jett Parsley, Elizabeth Moose, Chip Moore, Mark Franek, and Jessica Andrews, who have taken our strategies and adapted them to suit their own students and courses, thereby convincing us that we weren't being too prescriptive after all.

To Gerry Larson—librarian extraordinaire—for suggesting novels to connect to a study of young adult film.

To Nelda Caddell and Diane Kessler for providing us with information about current copyright laws and regulations.

To our friends at NCTE and the Assembly for Media Arts, particularly Rich Fehlman, Patti Slagle, Ben Fuller, and Andrew Garrison, who are passionate about film and its place in English studies, and who continue to share with us that passion and their friendship.

To Van Garrison, Gerry Larson, Mark Franek, Rachel Kleinberg, and Billy Fontenot, who responded to early drafts of the manuscript and made useful suggestions.

And, finally, to Virginia Monseau, who read our article in *The ALAN Review*, saw a book where none existed, and then invited us to create the book we always wanted to write.

Chapter One

Introduction

Background

In May 1985, Ann had two weeks left with her ninth-grade gifted class and she had run out of ideas. She was burned out and was at the point where she was even boring herself. At a loss for what to do, and looking for something new, she called Alan, who was—at that time—coordinator of English/language arts for the Durham County Schools. That winter, Ann had taken a film class taught by Alan at the Durham Arts Council, and she was hoping he would give her some ideas about how to develop a two-week unit on film that would perk up both Ann and her students. What Ann *really* wanted was a quick fix: a guest lecturer for a couple of days and then a few more days of film watching—a great way to coast into summer. What she got was a two-week unit on how to watch a film and write a critical review, and the beginning of a collaboration with Alan in using film with middle and high school students.

Alan, for his part, had taught high school elective courses in mass communications and super-8 filmmaking during the "media heyday" of the early 1970s. Most recently, he had taught film criticism to undergraduates at the University of North Carolina at Chapel Hill and to adults at the Durham Arts Council. Even though he was the English/language arts specialist for the school system, until Ann called he had never considered integrating film study into the regular English curriculum. When Ann called, he accepted her request. What he really wanted for those two weeks was to escape from the central office and have some fun teaching.

Ann got her unit and Alan got his break, but what we got that we hadn't expected was a tremendous surprise: students who, in that

1

awful last week of school, became excited, active learners—delighted with their new knowledge about film and the insights they discovered as they began to watch movies more carefully and critically.

This book is the result of ten years of developing lessons and teaching middle and high school students about film. The students' success with film reviews led us to increase our repertoire. We designed units on film genres, we introduced foreign-language films to seventh graders as part of an integrated unit on Japan, we applied principles from "reader-response" theory to develop strategies that encourage students to discuss and write about film more powerfully, and we incorporated film into courses in American, British, and world literature. As we developed these strategies, we began presenting workshops to other teachers at conferences and as part of language arts staff development in neighboring districts. The reaction of our colleagues convinced us that teachers were eager to integrate film into their courses, but they often just didn't have any strategy other than watching the film of a literary work and then comparing and contrasting.

When we present workshops on including film in the English classroom, two issues invariably come up. One is a widespread belief that students' reading is suffering because they are watching so much television or renting too many videos. The other is a variation of the attitude that "books are inherently more worthy than films"—often expressed as: "the book is always better than the movie." Before we go any further, it's important to address these two issues.

We acknowledge that students watch a lot of television. According to Jim Trelease in *The New Read-Aloud Handbook*, by the time children finish kindergarten, they have watched an average of 6,000 hours of television, and 59% of all teenagers own their own television (p. 4). Clearly, adolescents are spending time watching television when they could be reading. However, we believe that it's more the *way* students usually view movies and television—that is, in a passive, trancelike state—than the amount of time they spend. The strategies we've developed call for students to attend carefully while they're viewing, to notice details of visual and auditory images, to discover patterns in these images, to talk with each other about what they've noticed, to develop hypotheses and make predictions, to form opinions and evaluations, and to communicate their ideas about films. And when they engage with film and video in these active ways, they continue to develop many of the same skills we value in our literature curriculum.

Because we also want students to become lifelong readers, we continue to develop ways of exciting students about books, and we suspect that students' typical reluctance to read and eagerness to watch a video are the result, at least in part, of their experience of learning to read literature in English classes. Nancie Atwell addresses this issue directly in *In the Middle* in her sardonic list of "Twenty-One Things Teachers Demonstrate about Reading": "Reading is difficult, serious business. . . . There is one interpretation of a text. . . . Student readers aren't smart or trustworthy enough to choose their own texts. . . . Reading is always followed by a test. . . ." and so forth (p. 152). Our experience has been that when we incorporate the insights and practices of Atwell's reading workshop into our secondary English classrooms, students begin to embrace reading as something they want to do on their own time. We know many adults who are both avid readers and inveterate moviegoers. Students don't have to choose to be one or the other.

The second issue—the belief of many teachers that literature is inherently superior to film—is a little trickier. After all, many of us chose to major in English because of our love for the world's great literature—for its ability to transport us to other worlds, to delight us with language, and to stimulate us with important ideas—and these qualities don't immediately leap to mind when we're standing in line at the local multiplex or staring at the new releases wall in the video store. Who among us wouldn't rather be reading *Emma* or *Crime and Punishment* than watching *Rocky XIII* or *Meatballs 4*? In America, it seems, reading is considered a highbrow activity, while movies are for the masses. And if part of the function of school is to raise the general level of the nation's intellectual life, then it's no wonder English teachers seek to raise students' taste in reading and to discourage consumption of lowbrow entertainment.

In fact, from the beginnings of cinema a century ago, film writers, directors, and actors have produced profound and lasting works of art no less worthy of study than literature. Thankfully, the films of such giants as Griffith and Eisenstein, Chaplin and Keaton, and Kurosawa and Bergman have been preserved and are readily available for viewing.

Sometimes this preference for literature over film emerges in a particularly galling way. At one of our workshops, a teacher actually stood up to say that one of the reasons she liked to show her classes a film version of the book they had just studied was "so they can see how the book is always better than the movie." Though we resisted the urge to throttle this teacher in the moment, this apparently widespread attitude begs for a response. Granted, Golding's *Lord of the Flies* is aesthetically superior to the 1990 film version, and Mel Gibson might not be everyone's favorite Hamlet. Even the classic 1939 version of *Wuthering Heights* with Sir Laurence Olivier leaves out half the book for goodness' sake! Perhaps it's as simple as great books don't lend themselves to great film adaptations. Maybe authors need the breadth and scope of a novel, or the immediacy of a stage, or the freedom to explore the inner life of characters (something notoriously hard to photograph). However, there are many great films that have no antecedents as literature (Eisenstein's *The Battleship Potemkin* and Welles' *Citizen Kane* to name just two) or that have been adapted from decidedly inferior literature (John Ford's 1939 *Stagecoach*, for example). There are still other films that are fine adaptations of good literature (Ford's version of John Steinbeck's *The Grapes of Wrath* or Karel Reisz's film of Harold Pinter's screenplay of John Fowles' *The French Lieutenant's Woman*). We believe that we do a disservice to students if we consistently convey that film is inherently an inferior medium.

We contend that literature and film both have a place in the English/language arts classroom. Just as we ask our students to be active readers of literature and to respond to their reading through classroom conversation and composition, we also challenge our students to become active viewers of film. We challenge ourselves to select good films for our students and to devise strategies that ensure student dialogue about those films. Our experience has been that students do rise to the challenge and that they do read and view at a sophisticated level.

Rationale for Including Film in the English/Language Arts Curriculum

In the ten years we have worked with film, we have learned how powerful film can be in the English classroom—both as an object of study in its own right and as an adjunct to the more usual language arts areas of reading, writing, speaking, and listening. However, in part because of film's place as part of the "entertainment industry" and because some have seen film as the competition for reading, not everyone agrees that film has a place in the language arts curriculum. In response to these skeptics, we offer the following rationale for including film study in the English/language arts curriculum.

1. *Students have prior experience with film—almost all of it positive.* Nearly all students have had vast experience watching film and video, regardless of their prior success in language arts class, and they've all had about the same amount of experience thinking about or analyzing their experiences—that is, none. In this regard, using a film in class can serve as a great equalizer in a heterogeneous class, an opportunity for both the academically gifted and those who are accustomed to failure to learn something new together. One of the joys of teaching film has been working with students who don't expect to encounter anything

in an English class that connects to their world. Suddenly the teacher is presenting a "text" to which they can relate, and they find themselves really engaged in learning. Sometimes these students are visual learners who have been lost in a classroom environment dominated by auditory approaches (lecture and discussion). Quite often the best work these students produce all year is their discussion and writing about film.

In working with film, we have found that we can take students beyond what they know about film, which is often considerable in terms of story lines, plot conventions, and popular actors, and move them into whole new realms of experiencing a film. In every film unit we've taught, there has been at least one "aha!" moment when students learn something they didn't know about film techniques, or genre conventions, or the psychological and social nature of interpretation. What's really fun is that they don't know that they don't know these things, so they literally begin to see and hear things that have been invisible and inaudible to them.

2. *Film is already being used in English classrooms anyway—and often in ways that are a disservice to film.* Sometimes it occurs to us that the question is not: "Should film be used in the English classroom?" but rather: "Can't we do something other than show a movie version of the book we just spent three weeks studying?" On any given day, we can walk down the halls of just about any secondary school and find a videocassette player in use in an English classroom. All too often, what's playing is last week's book, and sometimes the teacher is grading the unit test on the book and the students are "taking a break" from the usual work of school (attending, thinking, discussing, and writing). Sometimes teachers reward students by letting them choose a movie to watch because they've so patiently endured the rigors of real English. Sometimes there's a substitute and the real teacher didn't send a lesson plan. Sometimes the rationale for using a film isn't clear at all. We're still wondering why that eleventh grade American Lit class was watching *The Lion King*.

By the time students reach high school, the "read-the-book-see-the-movie" pattern is so entrenched that every year—to Ann's dismay—a student will ask: "When will we see the movie of *Things Fall Apart* or *We Have Always Lived in the Castle*?" or "Is there a movie of *The Epic of Gilgamesh*?" Inherent in those questions are two assumptions: the first is that the students do not plan to do much hard reading or digging into the literature because the film will provide them with enough information to get by; secondly, the film will give the class some relief from the "hard work" of reading. Often what follows a book/movie combo is a superficial comparison/contrast that subtly

Figure 1–1

Tom Batiuk, *Funky Winkerbean* © North American Syndicate, 1989. Reprinted with special permission of North America Syndicate.

teaches students "movies can't do as much as books can" and does a disservice to both film and literature, portraying literature as the difficult business in the classroom and film as a frivolous experience.

The strategies in this book will provide meaningful ways to engage students with film that break the read-the-book-see-the-movie pattern.

3.   *Film is an art form that has a rightful place in the English curriculum.* We could argue that film—viewed broadly—is a branch of literature. Feature films are analogous to novels, documentaries to nonfiction, short narrative films to short stories, avant garde films to poems, and so on. Of course film has similarities with visual art and music as well, but by and large people go to the movies for the same reason they read fiction—to lose themselves in a good story. We've often wondered who decided that plays are "in the canon" of university English departments while movies typically aren't. Is it because plays are more clearly the work of one author? Because they are more often printed up and sold as books? Because they tend to be dominated by language rather than by action or by visual design? We could make a case that a survey course in twentieth century American literature is incomplete without *Citizen Kane,* or that every course in Shakespeare should include Kenneth Branagh's *Henry V,* Orson Welles' *Chimes at Midnight,* and Akira Kurosawa's *Ran.*

4.   *Viewing a film provides opportunities for discussion and writing.* Using film in the English/language arts classroom does not have to mean 101 minutes of downtime. In fact, a lot can happen in the classroom between the opening and closing credits of a film. We have found that films provide excellent opportunities for classroom discussion—and not just at the end of the film. We have given ourselves permission to

stop films for questions, predictions, or discussion and to use clips or chunks of films to complement a work being studied.

A large part of what we do in the English/language arts class is learn to discuss, analyze, make interpretations, and argue in a civilized manner. As English teachers, we have often been disappointed during a discussion of literature because not everyone had read the assignment; in fact, some days only a handful of students were prepared. Film, on the other hand, is an immediate and a shared experience—everyone sees it together and almost everyone has an opinion, an analysis, or an interpretation. In our years of working with students, we have learned that almost everyone has something to say about film.

In teaching writing, we use the common experience of film as a jumping-off place for helping students develop their writing skills. So often the key to getting good writing from students lies in the assignment, and film offers terrific occasions for writing. Students can write summaries of a film they've seen, they can attempt to persuade their audience by writing a review of a film, they can analyze aspects of a film, they can compare and contrast films or elements of films, or they can go beyond the film to create a missing scene or develop a sequel or prequel.

5. *In recent years there has been a growing interest in the role of "nonprint" media in the English classroom.* Fifteen years ago we had a pretty clear notion of what a text was: it was the words on a page. The intervening years have expanded the notion of what a text is. Our students today interact with a variety of media such as hypertext, multimedia, and CD-ROM, in addition to radio, TV, and movies. English/language arts instruction has always given students skills to cope with information in their environment; that instruction now needs to encompass helping students be discerning consumers and competent producers in a variety of media. If we are to have students become "media literate," a good way to start is with the thoughtful use of film.

Purpose and Audience of This Book

We are writing this book for English/language arts teachers in grades six through twelve as well as for preservice teachers, but we acknowledge that, when it comes to teaching film and integrating it into the English/language arts curriculum, we're all beginners. The training of English/language arts teachers rarely includes how to use film in the English classroom. Typically, teachers are taught to teach literature and composition, sometimes speaking and listening, but they are not taught to teach film. When film is treated at all in English methods textbooks, it occurs mostly as an audiovisual aid or as something to compare to the "real thing" (literature). Most English teachers love film and use films in their classrooms, but many of them feel inadequate about the way they use them. They tend to *show* films but not *teach* films. We want to maintain the integrity of film—to show teachers how to teach film in a way that honors the art and history of film—as well as show them how to connect film to literature and the other language arts.

This book provides practical, hands-on strategies that we have found successful in getting middle and high school students actively involved in responding to films. We describe in detail what teaching film in the classroom looks like, include suggestions for films and clips to use, and provide samples of our students' work. We will connect the study of film to the study of literature and composition and suggest ways that film might be used beyond the English classroom in other academic areas. We assure you that every lesson we describe here has been used in a classroom with real live kids.

Principles for Selection of Films

1.   *Know your instructional purpose and choose a film that fulfills it.* One of the most time-consuming and important tasks we've encountered in working with film in the English/language arts classroom is selecting the films we use with students. We've always begun with an instructional purpose for the film, then chosen the film to fit that purpose, making sure that the film chosen is one we can defend.

If the purpose of the lesson is to have the students produce a film review, we look for a film in which there are interesting things to discover about cinematography, editing, and use of sound. If the film is dull cinematically, we don't want to use it.

Often, our purpose is to provide a thematic link to a work of literature. In this case, we look for a film that is comparable to the literary work, but is sufficiently different to provide an interesting contrast. In looking for a film to complement the study of *All Quiet on the Western Front*, we looked at other war films, particularly those that were set during World War I. We rejected the film version of the novel as being too much of a repeat of what the class had just read; we rejected *Sergeant York* as not portraying enough of the horror of war. In the end, we selected *Gallipoli* as a film that had a comparable theme—the end of the idealism of young soldiers—even though the settings were in different parts of the world.

2.   *Select films that are both appropriate for the particular group of students and are "teachable," that is, artful enough to warrant class time and student study.* The key here is to know your audience. When we look

for books our students would enjoy, we read with our "teacher's eye." When we look for films to use in the classroom, we use the same approach. We have asked ourselves: Can you imagine using this film in some class, somewhere? If the answer is yes, we move on to the next question: How will this film work best?

Once we have a place for the film, we ask: What are the potential problems with the film? We have rejected films for having gratuitous sex, violence, or profanity. Some films bored us—a sure sign students would have problems paying attention. Occasionally a film would be too intense or too confusing or too simple-minded for classroom use. Choosing films for use in the classroom is always risky. We have been lucky in following hunches about what the students would like. Sometimes the films that have worked best with students were the films that we worried about initially. We held our breath when we first showed the subtitled *Musashi Miyamoto (Samurai I)* to seventh graders, but the students accepted it happily. What we have learned is that if films are powerful and if there is something in them to which students can connect, they will engage students.

3.   *Choose films that students are not likely to have seen multiple times.* When we teach a whole film, we prefer to use films with which students have little or no familiarity. For this reason, we often select foreign films (*Au Revoir les Enfants, Pathfinder*), classics (*Citizen Kane, Stagecoach*), and critically acclaimed films that didn't reach a wide audience (*A World Apart, This Is My Life*). As teachers, we know it's more fun to introduce students to novels or short stories they have not read before. It's also more fun to introduce students to films that they have never seen before—particularly films we know they are going to love.

We have learned that there are dangers inherent in using familiar films in the classroom. If most students have already seen the film, they already have an opinion about it that they share freely and ruin the film for other viewers; or, in thinking they know the film, they are less likely to see it freshly and are not free to predict and speculate along the way. Ultimately, we feel it is a waste of time to spend the days it takes to watch and discuss a whole film that most students have already seen.

On the other hand, when we use clips to teach film terminology to students, it often works to use chunks of very familiar films. Here students see portions of movies they know well. They know what to expect; they often can lip synch the dialogue. But what happens is that they see these familiar films in new ways. They come to recognize the "art" that has been invisible before. They know that the opening scene of *E.T.*, for example, shows the spaceship leaving the little creature behind. What they didn't realize before is that the camera move-

ment, editing, and sound all work together to create the tension and
then despair felt by E.T.

4. *Consider the rating.* The Motion Picture Association of America
(MPAA) rating of a film is always a consideration in our selection of
films for classroom use. Clearly, teachers should be cautious in their
use of PG-13 films with middle school students or of R-rated films
with any "under 17" audience. Some school districts forbid the use of
films with certain ratings. For each film rated PG-13 or R, we weigh
the benefits of using the film against the potential problems. We are
concerned about students' right to view as well as their right not to
view. We advise teachers to know their community, their students,
and their reasons for using a particular film—and to obtain parental
permission in any cases that might present problems. We choose films
that we can defend. We defend them first of all to students, but we
also must be able to defend them to the community. We are careful in
our selection to consider the maturity of the students, the school policies, and the community standards. Our inclusion of a film in this
book indicates we could imagine using it in a classroom and that it is
worth teachers' consideration.

5. *Hang tough.* Finally, we hang tough with the films we choose
to show in our classroom in the face of predictable opposition from at
least some of the thirty or so sophisticated and often opinionated
viewers in our classroom. We ignore students' automatic groans when
the film is black and white or when it's not one of their personal favorites or even the type of film they would have chosen. We take
films that students probably would have never selected at the video
store and "sell" these films to them. We've had occasion to use all
manner of films successfully, but the key was in the way we presented the films.

We've shown Japanese movies to seventh and tenth graders who
had never watched movies with subtitles before. The resistance lasted
no more than five minutes, because they realized that in order to understand what was going on, they would have to read those words on
the screen; but, more than that, they became caught up in the story.
Vince is an example of a student we won over. Vince was a student in
a tenth-grade class that was watching *Samurai I* as part of a world literature unit on heroes. Vince had no real love for English; he was a
vocational student whose career goal was to be an electrician, but
Samurai I struck a chord with him. He became so involved with the
story that he rented the other two films in the trilogy. We get a great
deal of satisfaction imagining the scene as Vince, looking for all the
world like a potential renter of the latest Sylvester Stallone epic, requests thirty-year-old Japanese films at his neighborhood video store.

Vince and others like him have confirmed our belief that it is possible to engage students in films they wouldn't ordinarily watch.

Legal Use of Videotapes in the Classroom

One of the most frequent questions teachers ask us is: Can we legally use rented videotapes in the classroom? Everyone has seen the ominous flashing "Warning" that appears at the beginning of each commercial videotape and cautions us that the tape is for "home use only." Fortunately for teachers, federal law does permit the use of copyrighted videotapes under certain conditions.

The educational use of copyrighted films and videocassettes is covered under the Copyright Revision Act of 1976, *United States Code*, Title 17, Section 110. Films, videocassettes, and videodisks—in fact, all audiovisual works—are treated the same under the law; our use of "videotape" in this section applies to all formats of audiovisual works. Educational use of videotapes must meet two criteria: the tapes themselves must be *lawfully acquired* and their use must fall under the *fair use* rules. *Lawfully acquired* videotapes include original tapes that have been purchased, rented, or borrowed and copies of broadcast programs recorded "off-air" from television. "Off-air" recordings have such stringent restrictions that we don't recommend that teachers use them. However, for those intrepid teachers who wish to venture there, we have included the complete guidelines for use of "off-air" recordings in Appendix A.

Educational *fair use* guidelines allow almost all activities that occur in "face-to-face" teaching situations. Specifically, the law states:

> [T]he following are not infringements of copyright:
> (1) performance or display of a work by instructors or pupils in the course of face-to-face teaching activities of a nonprofit educational institution, in a classroom or similar place devoted to instruction, unless, in the case of a motion picture or other audiovisual work, the performance, or the display of individual images, is given by means of a copy that was not lawfully made under this title. . . .
> —Miller, p. 11

A committee report from the House of Representatives (*Report No. 94-1476*, Section 110) clarifies "face-to-face teaching activities" as including a wide variety of "systematic" instructional uses, but expressly forbidding "recreation or entertainment" uses (Miller, p. 12). The House Report also clarifies that "classroom or similar place" would include a library or auditorium if such a space is used for instruction. However, showing a film as a part of an assembly "where the audience is not confined to the members of a particular class" would not be allowed (Miller, p. 12). Of course, schools wanting to use films in other ways may apply to the owners of the film's copyright for written permission and pay the necessary fees.

In short, readers of this book can rest assured that, as long as the films or tapes they use are "lawfully acquired," instruction based on the purposes we advocate and the activities we describe are clearly allowed under the *fair use* provisions of the federal copyright law.

Of course, federal law is not the only set of regulations that might influence the use of film in the classroom. We advise teachers to know both their state laws and the policies of their local boards of education. For example, in North Carolina it is against state obscenity laws to show any R-rated film to students under the age of seventeen, even with parental permission (Caddell). Individual school boards may have rules regarding the showing of PG and PG-13 videos to elementary and middle school students, about whether the tapes may be rented or must be owned by the school, and about whether particular films must be approved by a selection committee. When in doubt, consult the media specialist in your school or district; we've found that they stay abreast of all the laws and policies that apply.

Bibliography

Atwell, N. 1987. *In the Middle*. Portsmouth, NH: Boynton/Cook.

Caddell, N. G. 1996. Personal communication. 17 April 1996.

Miller, J. K. 1988. *Using Copyrighted Videocassettes in Classrooms, Libraries, and Training Centers*. 2d ed. Friday Harbor, WA: Copyright Information Services.

Trelease, J. 1989. *The New Read-Aloud Handbook*. New York: Penguin.

Films Cited in Chapter One

Information provided for each film is title, country (if other than the United States), director, year of release, MPAA rating ("NR" means "not rated"), length, and language if other than English.

Au Revoir les Enfants, Louis Malle, 1987, PG, 104 min.

The Battleship Potemkin, Russia, Sergei Eisenstein, 1925, NR, 71 min., silent with English titles.

Chimes at Midnight, Orson Welles, 1967, NR, 115 min.

Citizen Kane, Orson Welles, 1941, NR, 119 min.

E.T.: The Extra-Terrestrial, Steven Spielberg, 1982, PG, 115 min.

The French Lieutenant's Woman, Karel Reisz, 1981, R, 124 min.

Gallipoli, Peter Weir, 1981, PG, 111 min.

The Grapes of Wrath, John Ford, 1940, NR, 129 min.

Henry V, Kenneth Branagh, 1989, NR, 138 min.

The Lion King, Rob Minkoff and Roger Allers, 1994, G, 87 min.

Musashi Miyamoto (Samurai I), Japan, Hiroshi Inagaki, 1955, NR, 92 min., in Japanese.

Pathfinder, Nils Gaup, 1987, NR, 88 min.

Ran, Japan, Akira Kurosawa, 1985, R, 160 min., in Japanese.

Sergeant York, Howard Hawks, 1941, NR, 134 min.

Stagecoach, John Ford, 1939, NR, 100 min.

This Is My Life, Nora Ephron, 1992, PG-13, 105 min.

A World Apart, Chris Menges, 1988, PG, 114 min.

Wuthering Heights, William Wyler, 1939, NR, 104 min.

Chapter Two

Getting Started:
Teaching the Language of Film

A Framework for Viewing

At some point in our introductory lessons on film, we—somewhat grandly—tell our students that we are going to change forever the way they view film. While our words really are a challenge (almost a dare) to the students and do get their attention, we have found that presenting the study of film in a structured, sequential way does change students' attitudes toward film.

When we first began using films in our classrooms, we didn't change anyone's attitude toward film. In our early attempts to have students analyze what they were seeing, their comments would include a variety of elements, but mainly they would focus on character or plot. Sometimes they would mention theme, action, the presence of humor, or, in the case of middle schoolers, gore. Ultimately, what we ended up with was a chaotic or muddled discussion that never mentioned the cinematic elements of the film.

To give a structure for analyzing film in the classroom, we have developed a three-part framework for viewing that focuses on the literary, dramatic, and cinematic aspects of the film. The framework, as we teach it in the sequence outlined in the following pages, demonstrates to our students how dramatic and cinematic elements contribute to our interpretation of the story and characters.

Three lesson sequences are presented here. The first one introduces the framework to the students; we call it "Three Ways of Reading a Movie." Students practice applying the framework to clips from a variety of films. The second sequence of lessons includes strategies for having all students view a whole movie in class. The third lesson sequence provides a systematic way for students to write a film review.

Lesson Sequence One: Three Ways of Reading a Movie

We often begin this sequence with an informal film inventory. We give students index cards and ask them to list on the cards their ten all-time favorite movies. In the discussion that follows, we ask the students to comment on why those films are their favorites and what particular elements in the films they especially like. The discussion is always lively, with everyone contributing. What usually emerges from the student talk is that they like movies with compelling plots or memorable characters. We have never heard students say that they liked a film because of its fluid cinematography or effective editing.

Literary Aspects of a Film

We then introduce the framework for viewing, using the graphic organizer shown in Figure 2–1.

We begin with the literary aspects of a film. The literary aspects are those aspects that films share with literature: plot, characters, setting, themes, point of view, recurring images, and symbols. We point out to the students that most of the reasons they give for liking a particular film are on this literary level—they like the characters or the plot. The literary level is familiar territory for middle and high school students. They are accustomed to class discussions that use these terms for analysis.

To practice discussing a film on the literary level, we ask the students to look back at their lists of favorite films and choose one. Then we ask these questions, which students can answer in pairs or in a whole class discussion:

- Who are the characters in the film?
- What is the film's setting?
- Briefly summarize the plot.
- From whose point of view is the story told?
- What is a theme of the film?
- What is the mood of the film?
- What symbols did you notice in the film?

Figure 2–1

How to Read a Movie
(reading a movie on three levels...)

LITERARY
Definition:

DRAMATIC
Definition:

CINEMATIC
Definition:

It's helpful at this point to practice with some clips of films that illustrate literary aspects. Scenes from movies we have used successfully to practice identifying literary elements include:

Boyz N the Hood (John Singleton, 1991, R, 112 min.)
[0:05:05 to 0:13:45]

This scene begins as the young Tre is walking home from school while his mother talks on the phone to someone at the school. Key characters are Tre, his mother, his father, his friends in his father's neighborhood, and the person on the phone. Note the differences in the two neighborhoods and how the setting influences the story. Do any themes emerge in this scene? (Caution: there is one obscenity in this clip.)

To Kill a Mockingbird (Robert Mulligan, 1962, NR, 129 min.) [0:03:05 to 0:09:05]

This is the first scene after the credits. The voice-over narrator, Scout as a grown woman, describes the place and time of the film. Then we meet Scout; her father, Atticus; her brother, Jem; the housekeeper, Calpurnia; Miss Maudie; Dill; and Mr. Radley. The clip ends with Jem's comment, "There goes the meanest man that ever took a breath of life."

Citizen Kane (Orson Welles, 1941, NR, 119 min.) [0:02:55 to 0:12:15]

The second major sequence in this classic film is a newsreel biography of the title character, Charles Foster Kane. Typical of the newsreels of the day, there are screen titles and a voice-over narration that is by turns clinical, bombastic, and melodramatic, with a penchant for hyperbole ("the biggest private zoo since Noah"). The newsreel gives us Kane's entire story in capsule and from an objective, or at least journalistic, point of view. After this scene, the viewer knows everything that happens to Kane—our only interest from here on is *"why?"*

Raising Arizona (Joel Coen, 1987, PG-13, 94 min.) [0:00:00 to 0:04:50]

In the opening scene, Hi narrates three episodes in his criminal history, during which he meets and falls in love with Officer Ed. The scene is particularly notable for its wacky dialogue, inflated diction, mispronunciations, exaggerated accents, and silly jokes. (Caution: some mild obscenity.)

Dramatic Aspects of a Film

Dramatic aspects are those elements that film shares with live drama. We point out to students that films, like plays, have actors portraying characters. These characters engage in dialogue, and often the actors wear costumes and makeup that are essential in establishing their character. Both plays and films have sets (and, in the case of film, locations) that help the audience realize a sense of place, and both have someone who directs and puts a personal stamp on the action of the play or the film.

We ask students to go back to their lists of favorite films, and we use these prompts to elicit student comments on the dramatic level:

- Identify a movie you went to see just because a certain actor was in it.

- Which of these movies would you say had excellent acting? Why?

- Identify a movie in which the costumes, makeup, or sets were effective or unusual.

- Sometimes we notice dramatic aspects because of a flaw in a film. Can you identify a movie in which the acting, sets, makeup, or costumes attracted your attention because they were flawed in some way?

Some students may not have been aware that costumes, makeup, or sets contribute to the meaning of a film. Thoughtful use of clips at this point will help them identify dramatic aspects that contribute significantly to their interpretation of a scene. Clips rich in dramatic details include the following:

The Age of Innocence (Martin Scorsese, 1993, PG, 138 min.) [0:08:47 to 0:14:00]

The second major scene in the film takes place at a lavish ball. A voice-over narrator describes the interior of the house as Newland Archer walks through on his way to the ballroom. The details of the costumes, props, makeup, and decor (especially the paintings) provide information about the characters as well as the social background of the film. Students might also comment on the style of dancing and what that tells us about social conventions of the period.

Dick Tracy (Warren Beatty, 1990, PG, 105 min.) [0:08:00 to 0:10:18]

Note the details of set, makeup, and costumes (particularly the use of bright, primary colors). The matte paintings of the city add to the retro/futuristic look of the film.

The Magnificent Ambersons **(Orson Welles, 1942, NR,
88 min.) [0:08:55 to 0:12:05]**

George Minniver meets Lucy Morgan at a lavish party. As they move
through the house, we learn about the characters through the costumes, decor, and dialogue.

Popeye **(Robert Altman, 1980, PG, 114 min.)
[0:02:25 to 0:06:30]**

The opening scene of this musical film introduces the whimsically
designed town of Sweet Haven and its colorful denizens. Students
will note details of the set, costumes, makeup, and exaggerated action that give the film the feeling of a live-action cartoon.

Cinematic Aspects of a Film

Before we introduce the cinematic level, we often ask students how
movies are different from books or plays. We don't really expect much
of an answer, but sometimes someone will mention special effects or
errors in continuity. Students' knowledge of cinematic elements is frequently based on television specials like *Through the Eyes of Forrest
Gump*. Many young people are savvy about computer-generated images, blue-screen techniques, or matting and can explain in detail exactly how a certain film's special effects were done; however, they
have little experience describing cinematography or editing.

When we teach the cinematic aspects of films, we include technical terms that describe cinematography, sound, editing, and special visual effects. Teaching the cinematic level is exciting, because we watch
students move from what they already know to what they don't
know. Since students are least familiar with this type of discussion or
analysis, they need to know some technical terminology. Sometimes
we begin this introduction to film language by talking the class
through a list of film terms like the one in Figure 2–2.

Another option is to use *Basic Film Terms: A Visual Dictionary* (available from Pyramid Film and Video, Box 1048, Santa Monica, CA
90406-1048), which defines and gives examples of various shots, editing techniques, and sound sources. With this short film, we provide
a note-taking sheet on which students can list the terms they encounter (Figure 2–3).

Another resource for teaching cinematic elements is the final video from public television's 1995 *American Cinema* series (available only
by mail from The Annenberg/CPB Collection, PO Box 2345, S. Burl-

Figure 2–2

GLOSSARY OF FILM TERMS

A. **Types of Shots**

Long Shot–(a relative term) a shot taken from a sufficient distance to show a landscape, a building, or a large crowd.

Medium Shot–(also relative) a shot between a long shot and a close-up that might show two people in full figure or several people from the waist up.

Close-up–a shot of one face or object that fills the screen completely.

Extreme Close-up–a shot of a small object or part of a face that fills the screen.

B. **Camera Angles**

High Angle–the camera looks down at what is being photographed.

"Eye Level"–a shot that approximates human vision–a camera presents an object so that the line between camera and object is parallel to the ground.

Low Angle–the camera looks up at what is being photographed.

C. **Camera Movement**

Pan–the camera moves horizontally on a fixed base.

Tilt–the camera points up or down from a fixed base.

Tracking (Dolly) Shot–the camera moves through space on a wheeled truck (or dolly), but stays in the same plane.

Boom–the camera moves up or down through space.

Zoom–not a camera movement, but a shift in the focal length of the camera lens to give the impression that the camera is getting closer to or farther from an object.

D. **Duration of Shots**

Shots also vary in time from subliminal (a few frames) to quick (less that a second) to "average" (more than a second but less than a minute) to lengthy (more than a minute).

E. **Editing**

Cut–the most common type of transition in which one scene ends and a new one immediately begins.

Fade-out/Fade-in–one scene gradually goes dark and the new one gradually emerges from the darkness.

Dissolve–a gradual transition in which the end of one scene is superimposed over the beginning of a new one.

Wipe–an optical effect in which one shot appears to"wipe" the preceding one from the screen. Special wipes include flip wipes, iris wipes, star wipes, etc.

F. **Sources of Sound in Film**

Voice-over narration, dialogue, sound effects, and soundtrack music (underscoring).

ington, VT 05407-2345, telephone 800-532-7637). This cassette contains three programs, of which two are particularly useful. In the first segment, "Film Language," we see a director and film crew rehearse, shoot, and edit a three-minute sequence. As good as this part is, students will still need a background in basic film terminology in order to understand what's going on. The second program, "Writing and Thinking about Film," is useful in a study of film genres, which we address in Chapter Four. The third segment, "Classical Hollywood Style Today," is a roundtable discussion among several directors and critics about Hollywood's influence. (We've found this one least useful with students.)

Because working with these cinematic terms is so new for most students, we delay having them reflect on their list of ten films and proceed directly to practicing with video clips. One strategy is to give students index cards and ask them to list everything they see in a three- to five-minute clip of a movie. It's helpful to show clips of familiar films, since the students know the story already and can focus their attention on the cinematic elements of the clip. Sometimes we show the clip a second time (after some initial discussion), so that they can notice elements they missed in the first viewing. Sometimes we turn off the sound in the second viewing so students can concentrate on the visual elements. Clips with particularly interesting cinematic aspects include:

E.T.: The Extra-Terrestrial (Steven Spielberg, 1982, PG, 115 min.) [0:01:35 to 0:07:25]

The opening scene of the film divides neatly into two parts. In the first part, E.T. quietly explores the forest. The music is hushed and mysterious. Editing consists mainly of dissolves. At [0:05:00], humans arrive, and the style and tone change abruptly. Students are able to point out changes in photography, editing, sound effects, and music. They also see how this scene establishes E.T.'s point of view.

Dead Poet's Society (Peter Weir, 1989, PG, 128 min.) [0:53:28 to 0:58:00]

As the scene begins, the first student is reading his poem. A key sequence is when the teacher gets Todd to stand up. The photography up to this point has been ordinary (stationary medium shots and close-ups), but when Todd begins to spontaneously create his poem, the hand-held camera swirls around the teacher and student.

Figure 2–3

Basic Film Terms: A Visual Dictionary
(Pyramid Films)

As you watch the film, write down the terms as the narrator mentions them.

A. List three ways of writing a film down on paper:

1. _____   2. _____

3. _____

B. Two basic terms:

4. Basic unit of film structure: _____

5. A number of shots put together to show a single event: _____

C. Different kinds of SHOTS:

6. _____   13. _____

7. _____   14. _____

8. _____   15. _____

9. _____   16. _____

10. _____   17. _____

11. _____   18. _____

12. _____

D. List three basic types of LENSES:

19. _____   20. _____

21. _____   22. _____(zoom lens)_____

E. List five terms used to identify shots by CAMERA MOVEMENT:

23. _____   26. _____

24. _____   27. _____

25. _____

F. List five terms describing SOUND in movies:

28. _____   31. _____

29. _____   32. _____

30. _____

Figure 2-3, continued

G. List six (or seven) terms related to FILM EDITING:

33._____ 36._____

34._____ 37._____

35._____ 38._____

H. List four special effects or OPTICAL TRANSITIONS:

39._____ 41._____

40._____ 42._____

I. List two final terms:

43._____ 44._____

Henry V (Kenneth Branagh, 1989, NR, 138 min.)
[1:30:15 to 1:33:15]

Branagh's filming of the St. Crispin's Day speech masterfully supports Shakespeare's inspirational language. The low-angle tracking shot of King Henry establishes his leadership and gives scope to the event. The musical underscore parallels the rising tone of the speech.

The Road Warrior (George Miller, 1982, R, 95 min.)
[0:03:58 to 0:08:45]

In the film's first action sequence, Max outruns several threatening characters to scavenge gasoline from a wrecked truck. There's no dialogue, which enables students to focus on the variety of shots and sound effects, and on the superb editing.

Risky Business (Paul Brickman, 1983, R, 99 min.)
[0:07:20 to 0:09:33]

Joel's parents are leaving for a weekend trip. They give Joel instructions for handling the house during their absence. Throughout the scene, the hand-held camera takes Joel's point of view with the parents talking directly into the camera. Musical and sound effects cues are also noteworthy.

We now ask students to go back to their list of all-time favorite movies. For homework or in-class discussion, students are asked to respond to these questions:

- Is there a movie on your list that stands out for its photography or visual effects?
- Identify a scene from one of the movies that you now realize has effective editing.
- Is there a movie on your list that has interesting sound effects or music?

Putting It All Together

After explaining and practicing each of the three levels of analysis separately, we have students practice observing and analyzing all the three levels at once. One way we do this is to give each student an index card in one of three different colors: pink, yellow, and blue, for instance. All students with pink cards look just for the literary aspects in the clip, students with yellow cards concentrate on dramatic, and those with blue cards take notes only on cinematic elements. After viewing the clip, students with similar colors work together to compare their observations then report back to the whole class. Finally, we use the viewing practice handout (Figure 2–4) to guide students in their viewing and to facilitate discussion. We have found that we get better discussions when students have notes in front of them. Even students who are usually reluctant to participate in class discussions gain confidence when they have something written down.

Clips that contain good examples of literary, dramatic, and cinematic aspects include the following:

Batman (Tim Burton, 1989, PG-13, 126 min.)
[0:02:45 to 0:07:10]

The opening scene establishes the setting and introduces us to Batman and the typical denizens of Gotham City. There are many details of costume, props, makeup, and set design. The cinematography contains high- and low-angle shots, and there are numerous sound effects. (Caution: there is one mild obscenity in this clip.)

Psycho (Alfred Hitchcock, 1960, NR, 109 min.)
[0:34:50 to 0:43:45]

Norman Bates and Marion Crane share a meal in the parlor of the Bates Motel. On the literary level, in addition to characters and plot, there is dialogue about taxidermy, birds, mothers and sons, relationships, and "our own private traps." On the dramatic level, there are set details and props that convey the tawdriness of the motel. Cinematically, the scene is interesting for its mise-en-scène—the placement of round frames and curved shapes in Marion's shots and

Figure 2–4

Viewing Practice

Clip # Title	
Literary	**Dramatic**
Cinematic	
Sights	**Sounds**

Clip # Title	
Literary	**Dramatic**
Cinematic	
Sights	**Sounds**

square frames and stuffed birds of prey in Norman's shots. Also noteworthy are the low-angle shots of Norman when he becomes agi-
tated.

Citizen Kane (Orson Welles, 1941, NR, 119 min.)
[0:50:45 to 0:53:55]

Framed by an interview with Kane's friend Jed Leland, this sequence
shows us the fifteen years of Kane's first marriage in a series of
breakfast table conversations. On the literary level, there is the
framed narration, flashback, and the use of telling details in the dialogue. On the dramatic level, the costumes and makeup indicate
character development. Cinematically, there is a series of one-shots
with swish pan transitions to show passage of time. The musical
score is also notable. Bernard Herrmann underscores the honey-
moon portion of the scene with a romantic waltz; subsequent interactions are accompanied by variations on the waltz that fit the tone
of the marriage (jocular, sardonic, bitter, or chilly).

Stand By Me (Rob Reiner, 1986, R, 87 min.)
[0:36:20 to 0:40:50]

Four boys follow a railroad track in search of a dead body. While
they're crossing a bridge, a train comes, and the boys have to run to
avoid being hit by the train. Aspects of the cinematography that
make the scene effective are high and low angles, close-ups, and
telephoto shots with shallow perspective. The use of silence and
sound effects add to the suspense.

Benefits of Teaching Film Language

As students learn the language of film, they learn to analyze visual
and auditory images. Typically in the English/language arts classroom,
analysis has been confined to words—students have analyzed stories,
plays, poems, essays, and novels—but now their notion of analysis
expands to include more than verbal images. By and large, activities
in secondary English classrooms are not brand new ideas; they are
more sophisticated variations of activities begun in elementary school
when students first read "chapter books." Learning film language is
new. Here the students learn to see what has previously been invisible
and to hear what has previously been inaudible. Studying film language makes explicit the techniques for telling a story visually, height-
ens students' appreciation for the art of film, and increases their
awareness of how subtle cues can shade meaning. For instance, in
practicing literary, dramatic, and cinematic elements, Ann showed a
clip from the beginning of *The Road Warrior* and asked the class to say

something about the setting. One student said that the setting was Australia, citing as evidence the dead kangaroo in the road—a detail that Ann had missed in at least twenty viewings of that clip.

Even if all a teacher chooses to do with film is to show a film for the purpose of discussion, teaching film language is an important activity. Knowing the language of film enables students to become more careful viewers and to pay attention to visual images.

Lesson Sequence Two: Viewing a Whole Movie

After students have demonstrated some proficiency in using the language of film, viewing a whole film gives them an excellent opportunity to practice their viewing skills. We give students a form (Figure 2–5) to use as they watch the film and we explain to them that we will stop the film from time to time, so that they can reflect on what they have seen.

Some of them fill in the chart as they watch; some prefer to wait until the film has stopped to record their impressions. Stopping the film provides an opportunity to answer questions students have, to discuss a particularly vivid scene, or to predict what will happen in the rest of the film.

Choosing a Movie for Critical Viewing

In choosing a movie for critical viewing, we first consider how we want to use the film. Do we plan to connect it to a specific work of literature or to a particular theme? Do we plan to have the students write a review of the film? If our plans include a review or discussion of the film in a technical way, we look for films that have interesting cinematic elements or where the cinematic aspects carry a crucial scene. To test for a good cinematic scene, we ask ourselves if we would miss much if we merely heard the dialogue.

Before we show a film to students, we always preview the film. Even if we have seen the film before, we watch it again with our "teacher's eye." As we watch, we take copious notes, keeping track of time elapsed, main events, and notable literary, dramatic, or cinematic aspects. We also note places we might want to stop the film for discussion. We try to predict instances when we might need to clear up students' confusion. As a rule, we interrupt the film three or four times, being careful to stop between—not in the middle of—scenes. We also time the segments so that the end of the class period doesn't interrupt a scene.

Figure 2–5

Viewing Notes   Film: _____

Sights

Sounds

Events	Characters

Literary	Dramatic	Cinematic

We have found the following films to work particularly well for critical viewing with a broad range of students. With each film, we describe a scene in which the cinematic aspects are noteworthy. In some cases, we mention recurring or typical types of photography in the film.

North by Northwest (Alfred Hitchcock, 1959, NR, 136 min.)

Considered one of Hitchcock's greatest films, this spy thriller has several notable sequences, including one in which an airplane chases Cary Grant through a midwestern field, and another in which Grant and Eva Marie Saint hang from the faces of Mount Rushmore.

The Birds (Alfred Hitchcock, 1963, NR, 120 min.)

Even though this film is more than thirty years old, it works well with middle and high school students. Based on a Daphne du Maurier short story, the plot involves a series of unexplained bird attacks in Bodega Bay, California. One sequence shows birds gradually gathering on a school yard jungle gym unnoticed by Tippi Hedrin, but building suspense in the viewer each time the camera cuts from shots of her to shots of the birds on the jungle gym. Meanwhile, in the background, children in the school sing the same verse of a song over and over.

Empire of the Sun (Steven Spielberg, 1987, PG, 153 min.)

Recurring images appear throughout this story of a young British boy held in a Japanese internment camp during World War II in China. The film begins and ends with shots of the river flowing through Shanghai. Circular images include the rising sun on the Japanese flag, the window in the prison barracks, and Jim riding his bicycle around his deserted home in Shanghai and later around the deserted prison camp after evacuation. Of particular note is the scene in which Jim sees the cloud caused by the dropping of the atomic bomb in Japan.

Hope and Glory (John Boorman, 1987, PG-13, 97 min.)

This film, based on the travails of a British family during World War II, is rich in close-up shots that reveal the details of the lives of those who spent the war in London during the Blitzkrieg. Close-ups of young Billy disclose his wonder, fear, and sometimes delight in the changes German bombs make in his neighborhood and in his life. An especially interesting scene is a long dolly shot of the neighborhood after a heavy night of bombing.

After Viewing

Once the class has seen the entire film, we give students a few minutes to complete their viewing notes. We then ask some open-ended questions to generate discussion and to nudge them toward an interpretation of the film in terms of literary, dramatic, and cinematic aspects:

- What vivid visual images did you notice in the film?
- What vivid sounds or interesting use of music did you notice?
- What comments do you have on literary, dramatic, or cinematic aspects of the film?
- How do these literary, dramatic, or cinematic aspects give meaning to the film?

Lesson Sequence Three: Writing a Film Review

After the class has watched an entire film, taken notes, and discussed the film, the next step can be writing a film review. The film review provides an opportunity for students to demonstrate that they can analyze the various component parts of a film, synthesize their findings into a coherent opinion, and produce a sophisticated evaluation of the film.

Our approach to the review varies, depending on our students. With less-experienced viewers or less-confident writers, we ask the entire class to write a review of a film viewed during class time. This review becomes, in effect, a guided practice: we basically write the review together as a class to give the students confidence. Once they have the idea, we assign them to review a film seen outside class. With more-experienced viewers and more-confident writers, the film review is an out-of-class assignment. (Note: We always ask high school students to attach a note from their parents if they choose to review a film with an R rating. For middle schoolers, we require a note for PG-13 and R movies.)

What's in a Review?

We begin the sequence of lessons on film reviews by defining a review as a piece of writing that gives basic facts about a film and provides a summary, analysis, and evaluation of that film. The basic facts include the names of main actors as well as the key people responsible for making the film (director, writer, director of photography, or editor, for example).

We recommend that students write *brief* plot summaries. (For those students who need us to define *brief,* we say, "no more than five sentences.") We take the stance that the purpose of the review is to give enough information to let the reader make an intelligent decision about whether or not to spend money on the film; however, we also stress that the reviewer not reveal the ending or give away any secrets. We remind the students about that last scene in *Robin Hood, Prince of Thieves,* when Sean Connery appears as King Richard. For most moviegoers, Connery's appearance was a surprise, because film critics did not reveal his role in the film. Students have described to us the way audiences in theaters broke into applause when they realized who was playing King Richard.

We ask the students to provide a clearly stated evaluation of the film—their opinion of its worth or quality—and to support their opinion with a thoughtful analysis. In their analysis, students consider the literary, dramatic, and cinematic aspects of the film. We remind them that the analysis portion of the review will require them to use their new knowledge of film language.

Model Film Reviews

After providing our definition of a review, we give students sample reviews written both by professional critics and by other students. We get the professional reviews from local newspapers and from magazines such as *Time, Newsweek, The New Yorker,* and *Entertainment Weekly.* We save copies of student reviews each year and use them as models for subsequent classes. In selecting reviews to use with students, we are careful to choose those that mention literary, dramatic, and cinematic aspects in some detail.

Using copies of the reviews on the overhead projector, we work with the students as they identify and label the parts of the review, paying particular attention to the literary, dramatic, and cinematic elements mentioned by the reviewers. We ask students to write an L in the margin beside any literary comments, a D beside any dramatic ones, and a C next to cinematic ones. Sometimes they work in pairs or groups to identify the parts of the review.

Prewriting

When one of the follow-up activities to watching a film in class is to write a review of the film, we point out to the students—before they watch the film—the kind of information they will need to include in the review. We usually help them in their information gathering by providing a handout (Figure 2–6).

Figure 2–6

Gathering Information for Your Film Review

THE BASICS:

1. What is the title of the film?
2. Who are the main actors in the film?
3. Who <u>directed</u> the film?
4. Who <u>wrote</u> the screenplay?
5. Who was responsible for <u>photography</u>?
6. Who <u>produced</u> the film?
7. Who wrote/played/sang the music?
8. If you plan to mention any technical aspects of the film, you should find out the name of the people responsible for those aspects (such as editor, costume designer, and so forth).

DESCRIPTION/SUMMARY OF THE FILM:

1. What other movies is this movie like?
2. Who are the main characters?
3. What is the setting of the film?
4. What is the main situation or source of conflict?
5. Summarize the plot (without the ending!) in no more than five sentences. REMEMBER: Your reader wants to know enough about the movie to make a decision about going to the movie, but not so much that there's no need to go!

YOUR ANALYSIS OF THE FILM:

A. Literary Aspects

1. Characterize the plot/story of the movie. Is it involving, convoluted, simplistic, realistic, unbelievable, highly unlikely, well-structured, unresolved? (Add to this list if you need to.)
2. How would you characterize the dialogue? Do people talk this way in real life? (Or if realism was not a goal of the movie, was the dialogue amusing, poetic, or moving?)
3. What themes do you see in the movie?
4. Do you notice any symbols that recur in the movie?

B. Dramatic Aspects

5. Describe the acting. Did you believe that the actors <u>were</u> the characters?
6. Describe the sets, costumes, and make-up if these elements of the film's design are significant.

C. Cinematic Aspects

7. What did you notice about the film's cinematography? Did the director employ a lot of camera movements? close-ups? high or low angles? distorted lenses? special visual effects?
8. What did you notice about the film's editing? Were there quick cuts? lengthy shots? fade-in/fade-outs? dissolves? special optical effects like wipes, irises, and freeze frames?
9. What did you notice about the film's sound effects and music? What did they add to the overall effect of the film?

Figure 2–7

Writing Your Film Review

Look over the notes you made on the handout "Gathering Information for Your Film Review."

I. Plan your <u>Introduction</u>. Use a "hook" (an opening paragraph that catches your reader's attention). For example:

   A) Describe a scene, incident, or bit of dialogue from the film,
   B) Remind your reader of this director's last movie (or other movies of the lead actors), or
   C) Connect the movie to something happening in society today.

II. After the introduction, follow one of these two organizational plans:

   <u>Plan A</u>
   1. Description/summary
   2. Analysis*
   3. Evaluation
   4. Conclusion

   <u>Plan B</u>
   1. Overall opinion (evaluation)
   2. Description/summary
   3. Analysis*
   4. Conclusion

   * With either plan, be sure to mention cinematic aspects of the film in your analysis.

Arranging the Review

To help students organize their reviews, we suggest to them a couple of ways they might arrange the various parts of the review. We have them begin their introduction with a "hook"—something that grabs the reader and commands attention—and then follow one of two basic plans. This framework is particularly helpful for less-confident writers; better writers tend to get the idea quickly and run with it. We sometimes use a handout with guidelines (Figure 2–7).

Drafting the Review

Up until now, everything our students have done is prewriting. They have learned some film language, watched a film while taking notes, discussed the film, evaluated sample reviews, and devised a plan for writing the review. When the time comes to begin writing the formal review, some students freeze. Many of them love to talk about film, but writing seems a much more difficult task. To ease them into the review, we sometimes have them experiment with hooks for their reviews and share their hooks in small or large groups.

For example, with these ninth-grade reviews, Robin Crabtree's group agreed that her hook grabbed their attention:

> The quack is back! Catch this exciting adventure movie *D2: The Mighty Ducks* as soon as possible. The Mighty Ducks are back again and ready for action.

Shannon Dooley used her introduction to highlight some characters and aspects of the plot:

> Ah, the good old days. Chivalry was the rage, men fought with honor, and damsels were somehow always in distress. Oh yes, add some violence, a vengeful brother, an affair involving the queen and a knight, and yet more violence. What does this add up to? *First Knight*, of course.

Patrick Cheatham begins his review with a bit of dialogue from the movie:

> "Haven't you ever heard of the term 'dress for success'?"
> "Yeah, well, let's see here. They 'bout to turn off my phone, they canceled my credit cards, 'bout to repossess my car. I'd say I'm dressed for my success."
> This quote from *A Low Down Dirty Shame* pretty much indicates that money is a major theme in this movie.

Getting the introduction down on paper, with encouragement and approval from their peers, often gives students the confidence to complete the review independently.

Revising and Evaluating the Review

When everyone has a complete draft, students work in groups of three or four to evaluate the reviews using the chart shown in Figure 2–8.

The chart covers all components of the review and asks, in particular, for evaluators to check the amount of information included in the plot summary and to determine if the writer has written an adequate analysis of the literary, dramatic, and cinematic aspects. Using suggestions from group members, students revise their reviews into a final draft. At this point, the teacher also evaluates the final draft using the rubric shown in Figure 2–9.

Figure 2–8

Film Review/Peer Response

Readers/Critics: _____   Writer: _____

Point Scale: 4 = Excellent   3 = Above Average   2 = Adequate   1 = Poor   0 = Missing

Element of the Review	Points	Comments
INTRODUCTION • Did the introduction use a hook? • Did the introduction catch the reader's interest?		
SUMMARY • Did the review include a summary? • Did the author tell enough? • Did the author tell too much?		
ANALYSIS • Literary level? • Dramatic level? • Cinematic level? • Did the review include adequate analysis?		
EVALUATION • Did the review give a clear opinion about the quality of the film? • Did the author include support for the opinion given?		
QUALITY OF WRITING • Is the review well organized? • Does the writing flow smoothly? • Is the review free of mechanical errors (spelling, punctuation, etc.)?		

Additional Comments:

Sample Student Reviews

The following excerpts are examples of plot summaries and of literary, dramatic, and cinematic analyses from student-written reviews.

Summaries:

[Young Guns II] is a western set in the 1800's about Billy the Kid and his partners' struggle as they flee to the border while defending themselves against the law for murder. The plot thickens as a former

Figure 2–9

Film Review Evaluation Sheet   Name: _____

Point Scale: 4 = Excellent   3 = Above Average   2 = Adequate   1 = Poor   0 = Missing

Element of the Review	Points	Comments
INTRODUCTION • Does the introduction use a hook? • Does the introduction catch the reader's interest?		
SUMMARY • Does the review include a summary? • Does the author tell enough? Too much?		
ANAYLSIS • Literary Level? • Dramatic Level? • Cinematic Level? • Does the review include adequate analysis?		
EVALUATION • Does the review give a clear opinion about the quality of the film? • Does the author include support for the opinion?		
QUALITY OF WRITING • Is the review well organized? • Does the writing flow smoothly? • Is the review free of mechanical errors?		
EVIDENCE OF REVISION		

Grading Scale: 21 - 24 = A/ 17 - 20 = B/ 13 - 16 = C   Total Points: _____ Grade:_____

gang member, Pat Garrett, played by William Peterson, soon turns on Billy and is appointed sheriff.

—Laura Hayes, Grade 9

In [*Ghost*] Sam Wheat, played by Patrick Swayze, and Molly (Demi Moore) are a happy young couple with a thriving and promising romance. Unfortunately, in a sorrowful twist of events, Sam's life is cut short. Sam, who is now a ghost, must try to avenge his murder as well as save his beloved Molly from the man who killed him.

—Marie Wickel, Grade 9

[*Jurassic Park*] One day in the Badlands of Montana, a helicopter lands at an archaeological dig site with news that will astonish the two archaeologists, Dr. Grant (Sam Neill) and Dr. Ellie Sattler (Laura Dern). After a few minutes of conversation with the owner of an island off the coast of Costa Rica, the two are persuaded to visit what the owner, Dr. John Hammond (Richard Attenborough) calls a "no expense-spared-biological preserve." The scientists, joined by a chaotician and a lawyer representing the investors of Jurassic Park, board a jet-helicopter for the island. Meanwhile Dennis (Wayne Knight), a corrupt official who runs the park entirely by a computer, is persuaded by a company to steal a few of the park's dinosaur embryos. Everything is going well until Dennis makes his move and shuts down power to the perimeter fences and the fences surrounding the dinosaurs. To add to the confusion, a tropical storm is fast approaching and will play an important role in the plot of this movie based on the book by Michael Crichton.

—Jason Lugar, Grade 9

Literary analysis

Based on a novel of the same name by Pat Conroy, *The Great Santini* overflows with perhaps more conflict than necessary. Military life, coming of age, an oppressive father, death, and even racism are all exploited by the end. The subservient eldest son, Ben (Michael O'Keefe), who struggles to come out from under his father's clutches, is perhaps the only redeeming factor.

The story is original but hardly uplifting, and the effects are, for the most part, clear but nowhere close to eye catching. Even the sweet black folks who played a role in the southern town of the setting failed to be charming because they were so stereotypical, and Meechum's wife (Blythe Danner) had a bad Southern accent to boot. There was definitely enough unbelievability in the plot that I doubt any viewer could muster an ounce of empathy.

—Margaret Griffin, Grade 9

Although the plot of *Forrest Gump* is highly unlikely, it is very moving, showing how a small town society (Greenbeau, Alabama, to be exact) reacts to a man with a slow mind and a big heart. He is never really accepted by anyone, except to be called the "local idiot," but he manages to make friends like Bubba (Mykelti Williamson) and Lt. Dan (Gary Sinise) while trying to comprehend life as he takes each step. Basically, the theme is being in the right place at the right time throughout his life. He saves himself and his whole platoon during the Vietnam War, by simply following the instructions ("If you get into trouble, just run.") given to him by the girl he has loved since grade school, Jenny (Robin Wright).

—Betsy Holt, Grade 9

Although highly unlikely (impossible) the story [of *The NeverEnding Story II: The Next Chapter*] is actually quite captivating. Most of the dialogue sounds almost medieval. The only gripe I have about it is that Bastion said that he "must" save Fantasia. No ten-year-old boy is going to use "must" in that context in this time era. The ongoing theme of the movie is that one must look within one's self for true courage. The only recognizable symbol in it is that Fantasia represents all of the thoughts, stories, and dreams of our world.

—Bryan Taylor, Grade 9

Dramatic analysis

Another realistic aspect of *Poetic Justice* was the characters' use of urban dialogue. For most of the actors, their colloquialisms didn't sound as if they were desperately trying to get into an attitude that they knew nothing about. One criticism that I have is that character Justice (Janet Jackson) did not sound as if she "fit in" at times. What I mean is that in some parts, I could really tell that this woman didn't grow up talking too much slang.

Something that all the actors had going for them was their wardrobe. Nobody's clothes looked as if they were exaggerated so as to stress (or over stress) the urban flavor of this film.

—Hazel Ogugua-Smith, Grade 9

Jason Scott Lee brings [*Dragon: The Bruce Lee Story*] alive with his skills in martial arts and with his love of fighting. Lee was perfect for the part; he really portrayed his character as a real, believable person. Lauren Holly also did an excellent job playing the part of Linda. She had enough anger and hostility to play the part of a fighter's wife, but enough care and love to be a mother.

—Amy Briggs, Grade 9

As Meechum's wife Lillian [in *The Great Santini*], Blythe Danner makes an unremarkable performance—too sugary and plastic at times to appear real, and with a Southern accent like cotton candy. O'Keefe fulfills his role as the burdened son surprisingly well—the only strong character besides Bull Meechum himself. Duvall is the only shining star in this piece. His portrayal of a man whose vision and mind are blurred by the military, who faces death with valor, but can't take being beaten by his own son in basketball, is strong and unbreaking—marred only by a crying scene that he very nearly turns silly.

—Sarah Pitre, Grade 10

Cinematic analysis

The rapid pace [of *The Hunt for Red October*] keeps you tense and never bores you, but don't miss a part while you get your popcorn or you'll be completely lost. The movie's music blended into the background incredibly well and kept the mysterious mood hanging in the air. The special effects were very realistic, many of them actually being real footage from the Navy. In no way did it have that "cheap" look.

In the beginning of the film some subtitles are used because Russian is being spoken and it does create the atmosphere of communism and socialism. Now everybody knows that subtitles are a pain, but they were done very nicely and were easily readable. In the climax when the battle is taking place many jump cuts are used and you may become confused about what you are looking at. But even if you are confused, it all comes together.

—Carson Hayes, Grade 9

Close-ups and high angles gave me a sense that I was right there on scene watching [*Benny & Joon*] being filmed. The most vivid slow motion scene was of the first time Joon sees Sam. Sam is in a tree, and Benny and Joon are riding by in slow motion. This gives you a taste of what love at first sight might really be like. Though there weren't very many quick cuts in the movie, the places where editor Carol Littleton put them were very dramatic. In addition to the camera work, the sound effects and music played a big part in certain scenes too. As you see the first scene of a train rushing along, you hear an upbeat new age song "I'm Gonna Be (500 miles)" performed by the Proclaimers. Then in another touching scene of Benny at the train yard, you hear the soulful song "Can't Find My Way Home" performed by Joe Cocker. Not only was this the right music, but the sound effects were perfectly placed by the music coordinator Rachel Portman.

—Jennifer Taylor, Grade 9

The cinematography [of *My Stepmother Is an Alien*] is extraordinary. Without all the special and optical effects the movie would be dull and unenjoyable. *They* make the movie along with the dialogue. When you see what Bag sees through a fish eye shot, where everything bends toward the outside making it appear distorted, it makes this scene one of the best in the movie. Also, the lighting and the superimpositions throughout the movie are some of the other optical and special effects that are exceptional. Richard Benjamin employs many close-ups of the characters, many high angles like you are looking down from space. The film's editing contained many quick cuts to show confusion and anticipation.

—David Dawson, Grade 9

Complete reviews

The Gods Must Be Crazy, but the Movie is Funny

When an empty Coke bottle falls from the sky, a South African tribe's life is turned upside down, and a series of hilarious and unpredictable events begins in *The Gods Must be Crazy*.

One sunny day in the Kalahari Desert of South Africa a bushman is walking along when an empty Coke bottle falls from the sky onto his feet. He takes what he dubs "the thing" back to his camp, and his family finds many uses for it, such as a root grinder, a pattern maker, and a hide tanner. However, there is only one "thing" and the tribe find themselves fighting over it, something they have never done before; therefore, they decide that Xi, the bushman who found it, must return it to the Gods. Thus begins one bushman's journey to chunk an empty Coke bottle to the ends of the earth. On his way he meets a bumbling biologist trying terribly to impress a pretty school teacher and an idiotic terrorist trying to wreak havoc on South Africa. Through a creative screenplay by Jamie Uys, their misguided paths all meet at the end in a funny and exciting climax.

The beginning of the movie is like a nature documentary comparing the lives of the simple bushmen to those of modern man, but the movie itself is a complete original. The plot is pretty much ridiculous: a man going on a trek to dispose of litter, but the likable characters and the beautiful desert setting often make you forget that. The movie never drags, all the way from beginning to end, and the dialogue is very realistic with the occasional smashing one-liner.

One of the best parts of the movie, and certainly the most important for backing up the plot is the acting. The bushman actor, N!xau does a spectacular job of portraying his character, Xi. He never speaks English during the course of the movie (in fact, no one did: it was originally a South African movie, but it was dubbed for release in the U.S.), but his friendly and innocent mannerisms make you understand his character. Marius Weyer's character, Andrew Stein, is wonderful. Weyers does a great job of playing a man so intelligent he can identify any insect in the world by sight, but who, when in the presence of an attractive woman such as Kate Thompson (Sandra Prinsloo), is prone to set himself on fire and lodge jeeps in fifty-foot-tall trees. Louw Verwey, who plays the infamous terrorist Sam Boga, does a fine performance of a bad guy who can never get anything right. Good acting really keeps the silly storyline going.

James Uys—director, producer, and writer—used wonderful camera techniques that made the movie much more interesting. Most of the shots that involved people were one shots. These helped to emphasize what they were saying. He also uses the camera to set the mood. For calm scenes he uses clean cuts and dissolves, but when trouble is brewing you find yourself bombarded by fast motion, jump cuts, and fast music by Johnny Boshoff. Uys also uses freeze frames for important discoveries such as cobras and lions. The only real problem with the photography is that it really was shot in the Kalahari and the whole movie is slightly over-exposed.

The film is a wonderful reminder that new things do not always bring happiness, but instead trouble. The combination of intelligent and slapstick humor keeps the movie enjoyable and funny without being irritating. If you like genuinely funny movies without tons of decapitations and flying intestines, then you'll love *The Gods Must Be Crazy*.

—Ben Steere, Grade 9

A Little Something Wicked

"Y'know, I feel restless. Must be a storm coming." Jason Robards' character, Charles Holloway, aptly sums up the whole beginning of *Something Wicked This Way Comes* in that one sentence.

A storm is indeed coming. A flood of evil by the name of Dark's Pandemonium Carnival. Two boys, Will Holloway (Shaun Carson) and Jim Nightshade (Vidal Peterson), discover that the carnival is a twisted, dark mirror of happiness and dreams. All of the townspeople have their wildest dreams given to them, but with an ironic twist.

Although movies of the supernatural are often too unrealistic, the events that happen in *Something Wicked This Way Comes* fit into the plot so neatly that you barely notice them as more than shivers. It is other things that scare, such as the uselessness of an old heart, or the idea of paying for your dreams with your very soul.

The acting is superb. When Jason Robards speaks of death and regret, you can see it on his face and hear it in his tone. He makes you know intimately the weariness of Charles Holloway with one expression. Jonathan Pryce plays the owner of the carnival, Mr. Dark. He seems made for the part of this ultimate salesman of dreams gone sour. Pryce tells Dark's obvious lies, and gives his false smiles perfectly.

The film is very low lit with plenty of eerie long shots of the carnival grounds and of Main Street. But one of the real stars of the movie is the soundtrack. The music is very classical with an intense haunting mood. However, the real masterpiece of the soundtrack is the wind. Throughout the movie it whispers softly, sweeping leaves through the streets, howls with thunder and lightning intensity, and even wails like a group of lost souls.

Overall, this is a wonderfully scary movie. You can't help but get sucked into the philosophy about how badly people want their dreams, how regret takes a slice out of one's soul, and the trials of growing up. It also has only (literally) a handful of blood, but it also has enough psychological terror, unnatural events, and tarantulas to keep you on the edge of your seat.

If you want a gore-less psychological thriller, this is the perfect late-night snack to rent.

—Randi Storch, Grade 9

Jaws

"Shark!" Everyone pauses, terrified. Again, "Shark, get out of the water!" The Amity beach springs to life. Hundreds of panic-stricken swimmers hustle to the safety of the shore. Behind the jostling crowd, a tremendous dorsal fin appears. As the mob dashes frantically, the young and old stragglers fall behind. Muffled screams and blood are scarcely detectable amid the chaos. The gigantic killer has struck again.

Ironically, the "peaceful" town of Amity Island, Massachusetts, is shattered by several violent deaths, and police chief Martin Brodie (Roy Scheider) is forced to investigate. Brodie believes a shark committed the attacks, but Amity's stubborn mayor (Murray Hamilton) refuses to close the beaches. Closing Amity beaches on the Fourth of July would cause bankruptcy. After more fatal incidents, Matt Hooper (Richard Dreyfuss), a shark expert, arrives. He and Brodie charter the boat of Captain Quint (Robert Shaw), who has spent a lifetime chasing sharks. The three set off on a dangerous quest to destroy the massive predator. Their perilous mission aboard *Orca* results in a spectacular clash of man versus nature, with both sides trying to avoid the "jaws" of death.

Steven Spielberg (also the director of *E.T.* and *Jurassic Park*) has created a thrilling tale of a dreaded killer. Peter Benchley, the author of the novel *Jaws*, has helped to develop the entertaining screenplay. The most important factor is John Williams' haunting music, which grows in intensity each time the great white approaches, keeping viewers on the edge of their seats.

Convincing acting contributes to the appeal. Scheider plays his role as a confused landlubber urban police chief out of his element in this small town resort. Scheider is caught between the prosperity of the town (strongly backed by Murray Hamilton), and the safety of its citizens and his own family. Robert Shaw is a boat captain, full of fish tales and amusing expressions, reluctant to accept help from an argumentative scientist and his high-tech equipment. Richard Dreyfuss portrays an affluent oceanographer who shares a shark obsession with Captain Quint. The three form an interesting combination of courage, wits, and strength forced to confront a huge, unstoppable eating machine.

The model shark, Bruce, steals the show. Artist Robert Mattey, the man who designed the giant squid in *20,000 Leagues Under the Sea*, supervised construction of the realistic great white. The goliath model is, as Quint describes it, "a twenty-five footer, all three tons of him." Ron Taylor's pictures of real great whites are mixed with Rexford Metz's underwater footage of Jaws to create a seemingly natural fish.

In addition to special effects, photography and lighting are exceptional. Camera shots from the shark's point-of-view generate terror and focus on victims unaware of coming death. Close-ups of flesh wedged between enormous teeth and relentless black eyes convey the shark's killer mentality. High angles of the swimming mass show the shark's bulk while surface level views of an approaching fin are even more threatening. Lighting creates an ominous mood, for the shark is a night hunter. Not only are sunrises significant, but the underwater shots have an eerie, murky quality. The most memorable shot depicts the *Orca* departing on its deadly voyage, framed by a set of gigantic shark jaws on Quint's window.

The PG rating is misleading. During the attacks, blood spurts from wounds and shredded appendages slowly sink to the ocean floor. Men are swallowed whole, shrieking for help. Though the gory scenes are an appropriate part of the plot, the generous rating is not.

The themes of greed, courage, and the power of nature guide this high action thriller. The movie is an adventure full of suspense, humor, and horror. Speilberg's *Jaws* is irresistible, a fearful masterpiece that reminds all beachgoers to beware of the water.

—Lincoln Larson, Grade 9

Optional Follow-up Activities

After students have written a film review, we sometimes provide follow-up activities to the review, either as a final activity to a film unit or as activities scheduled later in the year that serve to revisit and review film terms and the analysis of film.

"Criticize the critics."   Since students have already taken the critic's chair as reviewers of film, we ask them to critique reviews of films by professional reviewers. One strategy is to ask the students to respond to a particularly critical review of a film. We make the assignment more interesting by choosing negative reviews of our students' favorite films. We consider the films the students listed as all-time favorites when we first began our discussion of film language. The most efficient way to locate negative reviews is to consult *Film Review Annual*, a yearly compilation of reviews, listed by film. We reproduce reviews of several films and ask the students to choose one review and respond to it. The writing is often lively as students defend near-sacred movies such as *Stand By Me, Lethal Weapon, Dirty Dancing*, and *The Breakfast Club*. Because many students take the negative reviews of their favorite film personally, writing the response to the critic also gives us, as teachers, the opportunity to review with the students the concept of tone and how to disagree without attacking.

A variation on this activity is to ask students to find a review of a current film that they disagree with and respond to that review. We can provide copies of reviews for this assignment or ask students to locate the reviews in newspapers or in magazines.

Comparative reviews.   Comparative reviews—reviews comparing two or more films—follow one of two plans. In the first type, students compare two current films with similar subject matter and analyze the films in one review. Examples of two such pairs of films would be *Wyatt Earp* and *Tombstone* (two 1994 films about the Earp brothers and the gunfight at the OK Corral), and *Braveheart* and *Rob Roy* (two 1995 films about Scottish heroes).

Another strategy for comparing two films would be an assignment in which students review a sequel to a film and compare it to an earlier film in the series. For example, compare *Batman Returns* or *Batman Forever* to the original *Batman*, or *Alien* and *Aliens*, or *Bill and Ted's Excellent Adventure* with *Bill and Ted's Bogus Journey*.

Films Cited in Chapter Two

Information provided for each film is title, director, year of release, MPAA rating, and length.

The Age of Innocence, Martin Scorsese, 1993, PG, 138 min.

Alien, Ridley Scott, 1979, R, 116 min.

Aliens, James Cameron, 1986, R, 138 min.

Batman, Tim Burton, 1989, PG-13, 126 min.

Batman Forever, Joel Schumaker, 1995, PG-13, 122 min.

Batman Returns, Daniel Waters, 1992, PG-13, 126 min.

Benny & Joon, Jeremiah S. Chechik, 1993, PG, 98 min.

Bill and Ted's Bogus Journey, Pete Hewitt, 1991, PG, 98 min.

Bill and Ted's Excellent Adventure, Chris Matheson, 1989, PG, 105 min.

The Birds, Alfred Hitchcock, 1963, NR, 120 min.

Boyz N the Hood, John Singleton, 1991, R, 112 min.

Braveheart, Mel Gibson, 1995, R, 177 min.

The Breakfast Club, John Hughes, 1985, R, 97 min.

Citizen Kane, Orson Welles, 1941, NR, 119 min.

D2: The Mighty Ducks, Sam Weisman, 1994, PG, 107 min.

Dead Poet's Society, Peter Wier, 1989, PG, 128 min.

Dick Tracy, Warren Beatty, 1990, PG, 105 min.

Dirty Dancing, Emile Ardolino, 1987, PG-13, 97 min.

Dragon: The Bruce Lee Story, Rob Cohen, 1993, PG-13, 121 min.

E.T.: The Extra-Terrestrial, Steven Spielberg, 1982, PG, 115 min.

Empire of the Sun, Steven Spielberg, 1987, PG, 153 min.

First Knight, Jerry Zucker, 1995, PG-13, 133 min.

Forrest Gump, Robert Zemeckis, 1994, PG, 142 min.

Ghost, Jerry Zucker, 1990, PG-13, 127 min.

The Gods Must Be Crazy, Jamie Uys, 1984, PG, 109 min.

The Great Santini, Lewis John Carlino, 1980, PG, 118 min.

Henry V, Kenneth Branagh, 1989, NR, 138 min.

Hope and Glory, John Boorman, 1987, PG-13, 97 min.

The Hunt for Red October, John McTiernan, 1990, PG, 137 min.

Jaws, Steven Spielberg, 1975, PG, 124 min.

Jurassic Park, Steven Spielberg, 1993, PG-13, 127 min.

Lethal Weapon, Richard Donner, 1987, R, 110 min.

A Low Down Dirty Shame, Keenen Ivory Wayans, 1994, R, 100 min.

The Magnificent Ambersons, Orson Welles, 1942, NR, 88 min.

My Stepmother Is an Alien, Richard Benjamin, 1988, PG-13, 108 min.

The NeverEnding Story, II: The Next Chapter, George Miller, 1991, PG, 90 min.

North by Northwest, Alfred Hitchcock, 1959, NR, 136 min.

Poetic Justice, John Singleton, 1993, R, 109 min.

Popeye, Robert Altman, 1980, PG, 114 min.

Psycho, Alfred Hitchcock, 1960, NR, 109 min.

Raising Arizona, Joel Coen, 1987, PG-13, 94 min.

Risky Business, Paul Brickman, 1983, R, 99 min.

The Road Warrior, George Miller, 1982, R, 95 min.

Rob Roy, Michael Caton-Jones, 1995, R, 139 min.

Robin Hood: Prince of Thieves, Kevin Reynolds, 1991, PG-13, 144 min.

Something Wicked This Way Comes, Jack Clayton, 1983, PG, 94 min.

Stand By Me, Rob Reiner, 1986, R, 87 min.

Through the Eyes of Forrest Gump, Peyton Reed, 1994, NR, 37 min.

To Kill a Mockingbird, Robert Mulligan, 1962, NR, 129 min.

Tombstone, George P. Cosmatos, 1993, R, 130 min.

20,000 Leagues Under the Sea, Richard Fleischer, 1954, NR, 127 min.

Wyatt Earp, Lawrence Kasden, 1994, PG-13, 189 min.

Young Guns II, Geoff Murphy, 1990, PG-13, 105 min.

Chapter Three

A Viewer-Response Approach to Teaching Film

From Reader Response to Viewer Response

When we first began applying the framework and activities presented in Chapter Two, our goals were primarily to provide students with a technical vocabulary for discussing films and to have them use the terms to analyze a film in a critical review. We continued to use whole films to supplement a thematic unit, but we did little beyond stopping the film periodically for discussion and clarification.

During this same period of time, we began reading articles and attending conference sessions on reader-response approaches to teaching literature. A natural link occurred to us: What if we approached films in the same ways we were beginning to teach literature? So we simply declared that we would use a "viewer-response" approach to teaching film in the classroom and we began to design activities from that stance.

As we have reflected on our own experience as students in literature classes, we realize that we grew up believing that a poem or short story had *a* meaning. A great work of literature *might* have some ambiguity, but there was always *a* theme, and any given symbol had *a* meaning. The author had somehow planted or hidden these meanings in the work. *Why* an author would do that escaped us until graduate school, when we learned that complexity, inaccessibility, and opacity were the key determiners of Great Literature. On any scale of reader expertise, we were naive at best and, at worst, too profoundly ignorant ever to develop an interpretation of our own. As readers, our job

47

was to excavate the meanings that the author had hidden—to work hard to unearth the interpretation the author intended.

Similarly, the teacher's (*professor's*) job was to give us clues, provide relevant background information, select the questions that would point to the hidden meanings, and tell us whether we were right or wrong. The teacher's interpretation was the right interpretation, because the teacher had taken a lot of courses or read vast quantities of literary criticism. It was the teacher's job to know what the author intended and to lead or push us to that interpretation. We learned to accept the teacher's interpretation passively and to regurgitate it on tests that asked us to "discuss" the meaning of the broken unicorn in *The Glass Menagerie*, or the unreliable narrator of *The Adventures of Huckleberry Finn*, or the patterns of color imagery in *The Red Badge of Courage*. The teacher was the ultimate Keeper of the Meaning, the final judge on the accuracy or elegance of any interpretation. We rarely remember hearing a teacher say, "What an interesting and unusual interpretation! I've never thought of that. You've supported your ideas with evidence from the text and your argument has convinced me to rethink what I presented in last week's lecture."

To be honest, we implemented the same practices when we became English teachers. Both of us remember laboring over study guides for the novels and plays we taught—study guides full of questions like: What is the symbolism of the rose in the passage on page 32? When Henry says "blah-blah'" on page 128, what does he really mean? Cite evidence that Jim is a Christ figure. What is the denouement of "The Gift of the Magi?" And the results we got were consistent with the approach: works of literature treated as fixed content, interpretations memorized rather than created, and readers convinced they weren't expert enough to analyze literature on their own.

Wrong:

As we learned to use strategies consistent with reader-response theory, we found that in order to produce empowered readers who could articulate their own interpretations and be respectful of others' opinions, we had to adopt a new stance as teachers. We had to give up being the only source of right answers, the sole determiner of relevant background information, and the final judge on all interpretations. Instead, we had to be a listener, facilitator, and consensus builder. Instead of *the* expert reader in the classroom, we had to become *one* reader among a community of readers. We learned to use our expertise to guide and clarify, perhaps to insert something the students had not noticed, but not to dominate the class with the "right" interpretation. We learned to postpone our immediate need to cover every possible aspect of the literary work in order to give students the space to develop as creative and responsible readers.

The application of reader response to viewer response was a natural development. When we read a text (or a film), we "decode" the visual (and, in the case of film, auditory) cues, simultaneously giving the words (images) meaning and creating a coherent and satisfying interpretation. The broad, long-range goals of literary (film) study is for students to continue to read (view) long after they leave school and for them to take responsibility for comprehending increasingly sophisticated texts (films). For students to develop as empowered readers (viewers), the teacher's role is one of being a model reader (viewer), promoting students' active engagement with the text (film), clearing up obvious misreadings, and encouraging clear thinking and articulate responses.

Viewer Response in the Classroom

Anyone visiting a class in which we are teaching a film using the viewer-response approach would see students watching a film on video and making notes on a viewing guide. Periodically, we stop the VCR and ask the students to jot down responses to a few open-ended questions. Then we ask them, "What did you notice?" They take it from there, and usually they have a *lot* to say. If necessary, we use the open-ended questions on the viewing guide to prime the conversational pump. Invariably, the discussion is lively, with most students contributing.

We usually don't talk much during these discussions. If the students ask us a question, we answer it as best we can. Sometimes we remind them to talk to one another, not just to us. If they make an assertion without referring to specific details in the film, we might ask them, "What about the cinematography or editing led you to this conclusion?" Occasionally, if no one has mentioned a particular aspect we think essential for them to notice, we might say, "One thing I noticed was X, and I interpreted this to mean Y, and I'm wondering if Z will happen." Through our comments and questions, our goal is to nudge them away from the easy traps of either their own immediate reaction or of accepting the teacher's interpretation without question. When we encourage students to take risks and when we accept a range of their responses, they in turn share more of their opinions and become more engaged in viewing and more confident in their discussion.

We typically spend five to ten minutes discussing each chunk of the film, unless there is a particularly controversial or ambiguous scene. Then we start the film again and view the next chunk. When we finish the entire film (usually after three or four class periods), we take at least one class period to discuss the film as a whole. Students usually complete a project or write a paper to wrap up the unit.

Advantages of the Viewer-Response Approach

Our reading of Nancie Atwell's *In the Middle* has influenced much of our thinking about teaching reading and writing through a workshop approach. In the same way that her vision of a group of adults sitting around a dinner table talking about books they've read provided the impetus for her workshop approach to reading, we have held a vision of a group of friends watching a film and going somewhere afterward to discuss it. In fact, our best experience of film discussion occurred in a course at the local arts council, in which a group of film buffs attended the latest offering at Durham's "art cinema" and discussed it over a potluck dinner afterward.

There is something powerful and immediate about viewing a film together and talking about it, especially in a secondary language arts class. For one thing, the students almost all actually watch the movie, something we sadly cannot say about their completion of the reading assignments in a novel. Ann swears that if she were able to hand out twenty-eight video copies of *Pathfinder* and assign it for homework, she'd have three students at most watch the entire film. But when she has shown *Pathfinder* in class, all twenty-eight students were on the edge of their seats by the end of the film.

The most obvious advantage of the viewer-response approach is that the approach calls for students to be active viewers—paying close attention to details while they view, writing down their immediate responses, discussing their interpretations with their fellow students, and supporting their opinions with evidence from the film.

In addition, using the viewer-response approach results in a much richer experience of the film for everyone, including the teacher. When students are free to express their own reactions and interpretations, there are often disagreements and arguments, but there is also room for surprise and delight. Sometimes it's even possible for the teacher to gain insight from students!

When we were first trying out response-based viewing guides, Alan did a "guest teacher" gig at a local high school. He taught *Citizen Kane* in a junior American Literature class during one period and in a senior advanced placement British Literature class during the following period. *Citizen Kane* is Alan's favorite film. He had seen it at least twenty times and had taught it four times at the college level. He had read books on Orson Welles and the making of the movie. He knew all there was to know about deep-focus shots, Bernard Herrmann's score, the radio techniques Welles transplanted to film, and so forth. He expected no surprises, but he was committed to trying out the approach, so he kept a low profile during discussions and pretended not to have all the answers so that the students would be able to encounter the film on their own.

The approach worked, much to Alan's initial chagrin. The students asked questions and made comments about details Alan had never noticed. "Why was there a monkey in that scene?" (What monkey?) "I noticed that everything was cold during this segment. Why is that?" (Well, there was snow, but . . .) When Alan asked the American literature students, "What figure from American history or literature does Charles Foster Kane remind you of?" he expected at least one student to know the "right" answer: William Randolph Hearst. Instead, however, he got some fascinating responses: "Jay Gatsby—because Kane is a romantic and thinks he'll be happy with another woman." "General Patton—because Kane just charges right on and doesn't stop for anything." The Patton response initially occurred to Alan as a bizarre answer, but the student's justification made sense and Alan took a look at how much of an egotistical bully Kane could be at times.

Once, a scene nearly provoked a fight. Toward the end of the film, Kane's second wife complains shrilly that he never takes her anywhere. Kane walks suddenly toward her, his shadow obscuring her upturned face. At this point in the AP English class, one of the boys shouted out, "Slap her!" When the segment ended, Alan turned to the class and said, "Obviously, something in this scene impressed you, Joe."

"Yeah, she was whining. I couldn't stand it. I wanted her to shut up."

The girls in the class couldn't let that pass. One of them spoke up. "Yeah, that's just like a man! He was abusing her! It's not *her* fault he has imprisoned her in that mansion!"

Joe wasn't fazed. "I still say she was asking for it!"

Suddenly the regular classroom teacher was out of her seat, pointing her finger at Joe. "Yeah, and you're the one who kept insisting Hester Prynne was a whore!"

Clearly these viewers were empowered to make their own judgments. To restore order, Alan asked, "So tell me, folks, what in the cinematography or dialogue had you have such different reactions?"

Using the viewer-response approach has resulted in our selecting films that we previously would have thought were too difficult, esoteric, or old. We have successfully used foreign films such as *Pathfinder*, *Sugar Cane Alley*, *Musashi Miyamoto (Samurai I)*, and *A World Apart*; films by such great directors as Orson Welles, Alfred Hitchcock, Louis

Malle, Peter Weir, and Akira Kurosawa; and films in (shudder!) black and white, such as *High Noon*, *Stagecoach*, and *The Maltese Falcon*. Students are more likely to give a film a chance when they are engaged in responding genuinely rather than looking for what the teacher will probably ask on the test, and students are less frustrated and pay closer attention when they have their questions answered and their misconceptions cleared up immediately.

The Viewing Guide

The single most important tool for teaching film using the viewer-response approach is the viewing guide. A typical viewing guide is a multipage handout with each page devoted to one segment of the film. Each page-long section of the viewing guide has three parts: a space for making notes on visual images, a space for making notes on vivid or interesting use of sounds or music, and a set of open-ended questions. Over the years, we have found that students enjoy taking notes in boxes, so we have designed viewing guides with boxes for visual and auditory notes. Figure 3–1 is a page from our viewing guide for *Pathfinder*.

Figure 3–2 shows a page from one student's viewing guide for *A World Apart*.

The guide provides a structure for viewing, note taking, and discussion. It becomes a record of students' viewing—a place for noting interesting shots, sequences, or dialogue. When they use the guide and stop from time to time for discussion, students do not have to wait until the conclusion of the film to discuss an image that occurred early in the movie. Using the guide also allows for more immediacy—students have the opportunity to address, in an orderly fashion, — any questions they have as those questions come up. Any teacher who has used films in the classroom must have had a student like Sharon, a student in Ann's English I class. Sharon was a bright student, but she always asked questions that made others in the classroom seriously question her intelligence. No sooner had the lights dimmed and the tape begun to roll than Sharon would begin asking questions: "Who is that character?" "Why did he do that?" "What did she say?" "What does that mean?" Before Ann started using viewing guides, Sharon spoiled everyone's viewing. Other students would roll their eyes, moan loudly, or shout at her to be quiet. Ann would find herself either talking over the film to answer the questions or stopping the film indiscriminately just to address Sharon's question. With the viewing guide, Sharon had a place to record her questions, and the viewing experience became more pleasant for everyone.

Figure 3–1

A. Wilder
Southern High School

Name: _____

Pathfinder **Viewing Guide 1**

Part 1: INTRODUCTION (10 minutes)

WHILE VIEWING—

Make notes here of any vivid **visual** images you notice:

Make notes here of any vivid **sounds** or interesting use of **music** you notice:

AFTER VIEWING THIS PART OF THE FILM—

What details do you notice about the landscape in this scene?

What could you say about the daily life of the people from viewing this part of the film?

What do you learn about the boy Aigin in this part of the film?

What do you expect to happen in the rest of the film?

Using the viewing guide enhances discussion in the classroom by including everyone in classroom talk. Because we view a segment of the film, pause to think and make notes, and *then* discuss, all students—not just the verbal, confident ones—become participants. All too often in classrooms the less-confident students check out and willingly let the eager ones jump in and carry the discussion. Having the chance to think and write before talking builds confidence and draws

Figure 3–2

Ann Wilder
Durham Public Schools

Name: **LINDSAY UNGEWITTER**

A WORLD APART   Viewing Guide 1

Part 1: INTRODUCTION (10 minutes)

WHILE VIEWING—

> Make notes here of any vivid **visual** images you notice:
>
> JUNE 1963 S.AFRICA   CAR ACCIDECT, BLACK
> GUS/DAD LEAVES   MAN HURT
> MOLLY AT DANCE CLASS
> DIANA AT WORK

> Make notes here of any vivid **sounds** or interesting use of **music** you notice:
>
> MUSIC
> ENGLISH ACCENTS
> TEACHER SPEAKS SPANISH
> DIANA TALKING ABOUT THE APARTHEID
> MAID LADY TALKS STRANGELY

AFTER VIEWING THIS PART OF THE FILM—

What do you learn about Molly in this part of the film?

MOLLY DANCES, WILL GO TO A COMPETITION
MISSES HER DAD

Why do you think Molly's father leaves?

FOR HIS JOB WITH THE ANC

What do you learn about Molly's mother in this part?

SHE WORKS SOMEWHERE THAT PROBALLY
HAS SOMETHING TO DO WITH THE ANC
JOURNALIST

Describe the attitudes of the white characters at this point in the film.

WHERE DIANA WORKS PEOPLE SEEM TO
BE FOR BLACK PEOPLE
BUT OTHER PEOPLE SEEM PREJUDICE

more students into the classroom conversation. The shy students who regularly—and often successfully—hide and let others take the lead feel less threatened when called on to respond. Even when students respond to our questions with, "I don't know," we can draw them out by asking them to share what they have written on their viewing guide. Our experience has been that everyone has something to say when note taking and reflection occur before discussion. Everyone has a role and everyone feels included.

How to Construct a Viewing Guide

We have found that designing the viewing guide works best when we divide the film into what we have come to call "meaningful chunks." We watch the film using a stopwatch or a VCR with a minute/second counter and we take notes as we watch. In the left margin, we record times. In the middle, we describe the action of the film. On the right-hand side, we begin to write our personal reactions: we make notes about striking visual images, we put stars beside important bits of dialogue, we write questions students might have, and we begin to formulate questions we want our students to consider as they view. Figure 3–3 shows sample pages of Ann's script of *Pathfinder*.

After viewing and taking notes on the film, we begin to divide the film into chunks. Each of these chunks will become the focus of one page of the viewing guide, so we are careful that each chunk is a segment of the film that is coherent and can stand alone as a "chapter" of the film. We pay attention to the time of each segment, but we make divisions based on meaning. As a result, some chunks may be as short as two minutes and some can be as long as forty minutes. As a rule, though, most chunks are from twelve to twenty minutes. For the sake of convenience, we usually give each segment a title.

After we have divided the film into chunks, we develop a set of four to five questions to focus discussion for each segment. Because we are looking for a variety of responses, we are careful to make sure the questions are open ended. Some open-ended questions are general enough to be used with any segment of any film. We have found these five questions to work with almost any chunk:

1. What do you learn about [any given character] in this part of the film?
2. What conflict(s) do you see developing?
3. What is the mood of the film so far?
4. What themes do you see emerging in the film?

Figure 3–3

Figure 3–3, continued

(6)

15.0' - Close up on Rask -
He is killed after A walk away   is
Knife w/ blood   Part IV pr

music   fade out

15.52 - New scene -   Part V
        Village -   17 min
        reindeer -
        Siege comes to camp of women + childr
        when an oth men? hungry?
        Mrs Rask know Varia?
        Siege says they'll take 2 days - they'll
        never discover the shortcut - The per

        inside shelter - women -
            go + wash - red sauce -
            making for the sauce -
            Argir leads their -

        Argin - Siegen we should never have left
            the log behind.
                ghost - It's not ghost we saw
                    fun
20:21   bird -
        A.gin - leading men -

22.13   new scene - in shelter - kit-
        new elders arm in arm -
        Ti - makes camp

5. At this point in your viewing, what do you expect to happen in the rest of the film?

Other, more specific questions ask students to speculate on the significance of a recurring image, to interpret a line of dialogue, to speculate about the motives of characters, or to point out details in the setting. Some sample questions that ask students to provide specific answers are listed here.

Hope and Glory (John Boorman, 1987, PG-13, 97 min.)

- How do you interpret Billy's refusal to tell his father goodbye?
- What do you notice in this portion of the film about the precautions the civilians take during the war?
- Describe Billy's grandfather's relationship with his daughters.
- From what you see in this portion of the film, who do you think Billy regards as the enemy?

A World Apart (Chris Menges, 1988, PG, 114 min.)

- What do you learn about the Roth family's relationship with members of the black community?
- If Molly were to write a journal entry about her feelings, what would she say?
- What details of life in the township did you notice?
- How do you interpret the final image of the film?

Au Revoir les Enfants (Louis Malle, 1987, PG, 104 min.)

- Based on Julien's conversation with his mother, make a statement about their relationship.
- What evidence do you have about the effect of the war on the daily life of the boys?
- What do you think is the significance of the phone call Father Jean receives?
- How do you explain the significance of Jean's statement: "I'm scared all the time"?

We have stressed the importance of using open-ended questions in the viewing guide because we want to generate as many meanings and interpretations as possible in discussion. That is not to say that we never use closed questions on our guides. Closed questions have a role when there is a fact that is essential to comprehending the film and we want to make sure they get that fact. To understand *A World* particularly about apartheid and the Ninety Day Detention Act. To give them this information, we either provide it as part of the introduction to the film or include it as a question on the viewing guide. A question that asks, "What are the important points of the Ninety Day Act?" ascertains that everyone understands the law that allows the arrest of one of the film's characters for ninety days without being charged with a crime.

Conducting the Discussion

In keeping with the spirit of the viewer-response approach, we are careful to limit our teacher role to that of a facilitator. First of all, we promote engagement with the film—we sell it to our students. If we are introducing a film with subtitles, for example, we present it enthusiastically and with a "can do" attitude that gives the students a sense that they *will* be able to read subtitles and watch for visual information simultaneously. Occasionally, we provide an introduction to give the students information they need to know to understand the film. Prior to showing *Gallipoli*, for example, we might give a mini lesson on Australia's role in World War I or on the geography of Turkey and Gallipoli and how the land formations might influence a battle. An introduction to *Empire of the Sun* would include some information on the British role in China in the nineteenth and early twentieth centuries and on the clash that sometimes resulted from two very different cultures occupying cities like Shanghai.

Often, no background to a film or its content is needed, so we simply begin by introducing the viewing guide. We tell students that their assignment will be to record striking visual images and interesting uses of sound in the boxes provided. In addition, we ask them to familiarize themselves with the questions at the bottom of the page and to use the questions to guide their viewing. We tell them that they may take notes as they watch or, if they prefer, wait until the end of the segment to write down their impressions.

Each time we use a viewing guide, we provide time for discussion after the class watches one chunk of the film. We stop the tape, give the students time to make notes on their viewing guides, and then start the discussion. We typically begin by asking our students to talk about what they have seen—what struck them visually about that segment of the film. We ask, "What did you see in this part of the film?" Because they have had time to fill in the visual box on the viewing guide, the responses are usually numerous. From there, we go on to discuss the use of sound and music, and then we look at the open-ended questions. Finally, we ask students what questions they have after viewing that part of the film.

In the discussion, the teacher becomes *one* viewer and not the only authority in the room. The role of one viewer is not always a comfortable one for us. Sometimes we know a film so well that we want our students to notice a particular image or nuance in the film. As a result, we have to bite our tongues to keep ourselves *in* our viewer role and *out of* our teacher role. We have solved this dilemma by filling in our own viewing guides. If no one else mentions "our" image, we bring it up by saying, "One thing I noticed was that the crow was flying overhead just before the enemy attack. I wonder if anyone else noticed that and might guess what it means."

What follows is a transcript of a conversation that took place in Ann's classroom following the viewing of the first twenty minutes of *Empire of the Sun*. Ann begins by drawing students out on what they have seen.

Teacher: Look in your visual box. What is one thing you noticed? Yes, Jeff?

Jeff: Coffins in the water.

T: Coffins in the water at the very beginning. Yes. Something else?

Jared: Airplanes.

T: Where, Jared?

Jared: In the air.

T: Where, in what scene?

Jared: When he's in the yard, he looks up and sees Japanese planes.

T: Yes, he looks up and sees a plane and says, "That's a Japanese plane." Before I go on, did anyone notice planes anywhere else in here?

Class: Oh, yeah! Everywhere.

Ben: Hanging from the ceiling in his room.

T: Yes, he went to bed and they were all up there. Was there anywhere else you saw a plane?

Renee: When he was chasing the toy airplane and saw the real one crashed.

T: Over the hill at the party?

Renee: Yes.

T: Can you think of any other planes you saw?

Dotty: The one that was going around burning.

T: Yes, the glider he held when the servant was chasing him.

Then, Ann encourages the students to say what these visual images mean.

T: In the first twenty minutes of this film, you have seen all these planes. Does that tell you something?

Class: Yes. Certainly.

Patrick: I think he likes planes.

Ben: I think he's obsessed with planes.

T: He seems obsessed, doesn't he? Something else you saw?

Ben: A close-up on the hood ornament on the car. I don't know if anyone else saw that . . . the little swan thing.

T: What is that? What kind of car is that?

Ben: Rolls.

T: Rolls Royce, yes.

Aaron: I saw the bum on the street.

T: Yes, the beggar. Something else?

Dotty: There seems to be a theme of fires.

T: Fires? Where?

Dotty: When his airplane was on fire and there's something else: when his father was burning things and they closed in on the fire.

T: Good notice. His father was putting things in the fireplace. What do you think he was doing?

Patrick: Burning documents. Things he shouldn't have.

T: Things he shouldn't have? Does someone else want to say something about this?

Randi: Burning things that somebody else shouldn't get to.

Ann now directs the discussion—and the students' attention—to a specific aspect of the film.

T: What is happening now, politically, in Shanghai?

Class: War.

T: Who is getting ready to attack?

Class: The Japanese.

Randi: So maybe it's something he doesn't want the Japanese to get.

T: Good. Somebody else. What'd you see?

Renee: The crowd on the street.

T: Yes, the crowd on the street. One note I had on my sheet was the contrast. You had the people in the cars. What were they like?

Class: Rich. Snobs.

T: Where were they going?

Class: A party. A costume ball.

T: Did you notice the costumes? What were they dressed as?

Class: Clowns. Emperors. Sinbad. Pirates.

T: Did anyone notice that one woman with the wig?

Class: Yes.

T: Who was she supposed to be?

Randi: Marie Antoinette.

T: I thought that, too. And what's happening outside that car?

Ben: People are being beaten.

T: Beaten. What else? Willie?

Willie: What's that thing that kept hitting the car?

Patrick: It was a chicken.

T: Yes, it may have been a chicken someone was taking to market.

Ann was pleased that in the next part of the conversation, students spontaneously began pointing toward cinematic elements of the film.

Samantha: And that little kid who was trying to run up to the car and was trying to tell them something.

T: The one who kept saying, "No mama, no papa"?

Patrick: I think we will see him again because they kept looking back at him. The camera was tracking him.

T: So you think he's important because the camera stayed on him so long?

Patrick: They were looking at him for a reason.

T: Good, Patrick. Anything else you saw? Yes, Ben?

Ben: Lots of different people's faces in reflections.

T: OK, give examples.

Ben: They did it with the faces of the drivers in the mirrors of the cars. And they put the kid behind glass a lot. In the car you could see his reflection in the glass.

Dotty: I saw the Japanese flag.

T: Yes, it was one of the first things you saw in the film: that circle blowing in the wind. Then you see the river. OK, ya'll have good eyes here.

The conversation now moves on to a discussion of sounds and music as Ann asks the students to share notes they took about sounds.

T: Now, what are some things you heard? Aaron?

Aaron: At first I heard a girl singing, but it turned out that it was a boy.

T: Yes, a boy soprano.

Ben: At the very beginning I heard water rushing.

T: The noise of water in the river?

Ben: Yes.

Willie: I heard when the ship came through and hit one of those coffins.

T: Yes, that clunk.

Ben: I heard silence. When the kid throws his airplane over the hill, and he goes to find it, the whole Japanese army is looking. There is no sound at all.

T: Yes, instead of mood music, there's nothing. Does that silence suggest anything?

Class: Yeah.

Patrick's question drives the next part of the conversation and the discussion is momentarily diverted from the issue of the film's sounds.

Patrick: Did anyone know the Japanese were over there?

T: Did you get the feeling they were surprised?

Dotty: I thought it was that the father knew that they were there and that they were defending the country. It was like he was saying, "Don't say anything, don't say anything, you didn't see this."

Patrick: So probably no one knew they were over there?

T: I got the feeling it was a surprise, but the adults may have known. How do you all feel?

Patrick: But if the adults knew they were just sitting there waiting to attack the city, wouldn't they go get them?

T: Did anyone hear the news report when his father was putting papers in the fire?

Class: Yes.

T: What did it say?

Betsy: It said something about peace talks failing in Washington.

T: And it said that one-third of the British nationals had left in the past few weeks. Many of these people are wealthy and have businesses, and they are worried that their businesses may be in trouble, so they are leaving.

Jeff: You can tell they make a lot of money, because when his father is playing golf, he uses a coin as a tee.

Daniel: I noticed when they were in the street you didn't just hear Chinese being yelled out, you heard English a lot, too. So I was thinking that not all the English people who live over there are rich.

T: So there were poorer people, good notice there!

Betsy: I know how you could tell they were rich. When they were driving through the streets, they were the only ones with cars. Everyone else is walking or they had bicycles.

T: That made it hard to get through the streets. It was as if they weren't used to cars, wasn't it?

Betsy: That's why they were beating them off their cars.

Ann now directs the conversation back to cinematic elements.

T: Let's go back. Didn't Aaron or Jared mention the beggar? Did anyone notice the noise he was making?

Monica: He was hitting the sidewalk.

T: All right, let's look at the questions.

Later in the movie, after viewing the second segment, the students and Ann share interpretations.

T: Something you noticed in this part, something visual? Ben?

Ben: I saw a lot of fog in the beginning.

T: Fog in that beginning part?

Ben: The light was dim; it was dark and underexposed.

Patrick: I thought it was just night.

Betsy: I noticed that when they were leaving the party and going back into Shanghai, there were more cars going out of Shanghai than there were going into it.

T: What you're saying is that people are getting out of Shanghai for some reason?

Daniel: I noticed that when they closed the gate on all the cars, there was barbed wire on the fences.

T: So maybe that gave you an eerie feeling like something was going to happen.

Willie: The boy was playing with his little light and he sees the other light, and he thinks it's the Chinese signaling back.

T: Let's talk about that. Were they seeing his light?

Class: Yes.

Willie: He thought it was funny, so he kept on clicking it.

T: Was his light the cause of the explosion?

Class: Yes.

Randi: I think he started the war.

Patrick: I don't think he so much started the war. The ship was right there and the war was going to start sooner or later. He just gave them a target to hit, because I noticed it hit real near his house.

T: Were they near his house?

Patrick: I mean the hotel.

T: My interpretation of this—and ya'll don't have to agree with me—my interpretation is that he was just doing it, and I'm not sure that caused anything. He's an arrogant type of kid and thinks he started the war, but actually it was just a coincidence.

Betsy: I don't think he really realizes what he does, but it's just that he doesn't care about it. He just does it just because he wanted to do something, and he didn't realize what he had done. He was just having fun and playing around. And I noticed that when all the planes and tanks were flying overhead and getting ready to attack and people were running in the street, he was smiling. He was looking down on them.

T: Yes, more arrogance.

In our classroom conversations, we may occasionally have to clear up a student's obvious misreading of the film, but our role is primarily to encourage. We work to include as many students as possible in the discussion by drawing out reluctant students, we use active listening to promote clear thinking and articulate responses. We often repeat the students' comments to give them a chance to hear what they've said, to affirm their opinion, or to restate their ideas in a way that more accurately reflects their intended meaning. We work to help our students create their own meaning.

Discussing the Whole Film

After viewing the whole film by segments, we promote discussion of the film as a whole. We have found it useful to have students prepare for the discussion by reading back over their viewing guides and considering several questions. (We have also typed these as a handout and had students write out the answers as homework.)

These six questions work with any film:

1. What changes did you notice in the film as you watched? What changes did you notice in your feelings or opinions as you watched?

2. Go back over your viewing guides and look at your "visual images" and "sounds" notations. Do you notice any patterns emerging? (For example, do you see the same images again and again? Do you hear musical phrases or lines of dialogue repeated?) What do you think the director was trying to communicate by using these patterns?

3. Make a list of all the things that this film is about.

4. Make a list of all the conflicts you have seen in this film.

5. What characters, incidents, or objects in this film remind you of other stories you have read or movies you have seen?

6. In your opinion, is this film neutral or does it clearly take a particular position on an issue?

The following questions are useful with particular types of films:

1. *For any American film:* What do we learn about the American experience from this film?

2. *For foreign and historical films*: What have you learned about the culture of the people in this time and place by watching this film?

3. *When students view more than one film by the same director*: In what way is this film similar to other films by this director? In what ways is it different?

4. *When the film is part of a thematic unit*: What does this film have to say about the theme we have been studying in this unit?

In addition to these generic questions, we create a list of questions for the specific film. Often these questions are based on issues that have emerged in discussion during the viewing of the film. A question from *A World Apart*, for example, asks students if Diana Roth is a good parent. After a viewing of *Gallipoli*, students consider the changes war has brought to two young Australian soldiers. Sometimes we use questions that connect the film to literature the class has studied. For instance, we use *Pathfinder* to supplement a unit on myths, legends, and heroes, in which we specifically teach the concept of archetypes. After they have seen *Pathfinder*, we ask students to list all the archetypes they have noticed in that film.

Occasionally we ask students to respond to questions that tie the film to a novel the class has studied, to a theme in the film, or to a concept a film explores. When we pair *Gallipoli* with *All Quiet on the Western Front*, we ask students to compare and contrast the experiences of the Australian soldiers in the film with those of the German soldiers in the novel. With *Musashi Miyamoto (Samurai I)*, we ask students to comment on themes of responsibility and maturity. When we use *My Brilliant Career*, we examine the choices women have today with those more limited choices Sybilla has in late nineteenth-century Australia.

After the students look back over their viewing guides and complete their responses to the questions, we discuss their answers. Sometimes we conduct a whole class discussion, giving everyone a chance to contribute and to expand their answers by writing down ideas that emerge in the discussion. On other occasions, we use a jigsaw activity and create expert groups that can return to their home groups to lead a discussion of two or three of the questions. Sometimes we simply ask students to pair up and share responses.

Writing Activities

When we first began teaching a whole film using the viewer-response approach, we were content to use both the viewing guide and the discussion that the guide prompted as end products. Then we realized that watching the film using the viewing guide, discussing the film at planned intervals, and reflecting at the conclusion of the film can be the early stages—the brainstorming portion—of the composing process. Knowing that students produce better writing when they have something to say, and knowing that they all had plenty to say about the films they watched in class, we began to develop writing assignments based on their viewing responses. Now our students write analytical essays on the films they watch, but they also produce imaginative, creative pieces, and they write personal essays.

Personal Essays

When our students write personal essays following the class viewing and discussion of a whole film, the essays frequently take the form of a letter. The letter can simply be a letter to the teacher reflecting on an aspect of the film, or on how the film affected or changed the student. Sometimes the students connect something in the film—a character, a theme, a conflict—with something in their lives.

The following are sample assignments for personal essays:

1. Write a letter to your teacher in which you respond to one of the following:
   - Reflect on one aspect of the film that you felt was significant in some way.
   - Explain how your viewing of the film changed or affected you in some way.
   - Explain how something in your viewing of the film—a character, theme, or conflict, for example—connects with something in your life.

2. Write a letter to the director of the film or to the writer of the film's screenplay. This letter may be congratulatory or critical, but it is important that you support your thesis with specific details from the film. If you decide to disagree, do so without being disagreeable. Watch your tone.

3. Read a review of the film and write a letter to the reviewer in which you respond to the reviewer's opinion of the film. Remember to support your ideas with details from the film and from the review, and to use the appropriate tone.

Analytical Essays

In writing the analytical essay, we build on the classroom discussion that evolved during and after viewing. We brainstorm possible topics as a class, then students develop—often as a homework assignment—a thesis statement. For some groups of students, we check the thesis statement to make sure it is a topic that will be manageable. For others, we provide less structure. In the next step, we ask the students to brainstorm supporting ideas for their thesis statement and to collect evidence to support their ideas from their viewing guides. Students then write a first draft that the class critiques in pairs or small groups. Typical topics for analytical essays could include:

1. Examine the concept of people's mistreatment of each other as shown in *Au Revoir les Enfants*. Then, develop a thesis in which you decide whether the film presents a positive or negative view of humanity.

2. Examine the interviews in *Citizen Kane*. Then, develop a thesis that explains why the filmmakers placed the interviews in that order.

3. Explain the significance of Rosebud in *Citizen Kane*. Is the word important to the film or is it a red herring?

4. Think of all the instances circles are used in *Empire of the Sun*. Then develop a thesis that explains what these circles could mean in the film.

5. *Rebel Without a Cause* is a film about teenagers who are in some way rebels. Develop a thesis that analyzes the types of rebellion that appear in that film.

Imaginative Writing

Imaginative writing assignments ask students to go beyond the film. For instance, in teaching world literature to tenth graders, we ask our students—with each piece of literature we study—to articulate what they have learned about the culture from reading its literature. We discuss what we learn about the lives, values, and beliefs of the ancient Hebrews from reading Old Testament literature or what we can learn about the ancient Sumerians from reading *The Epic of Gilgamesh*, or what *Things Fall Apart* teaches us about the values of the Ibo people of the late nineteenth century. We have designed writing assignments that ask the students to work with this same concept, but to "work backward" from what they learn about a society's culture in the film and create a hypothetical work of literature that might have come from that culture.

1. Imagine that archeologists have found a manuscript from the Lapp people of *Pathfinder*. From what you have learned about these people in your viewing of the film, decide what type of literature that manuscript might contain. For example, will it be poetry, a legend, a myth, or a personal journal? Then write the poem, legend, myth, or journal as it might be translated by scholars from the original Lappish.

2. At the end of *Gallipoli*, just before the final battle, we see the soldiers writing letters to be left behind in the trenches. Write two letters—one from an officer and one from a soldier. Think before you write. What details would each include? How would the letters be different? What would they say to their loved ones?

Writing Film Treatments, Scripts, and Storyboards

According to *Basic Film Terms: A Visual Dictionary* (available from Pyramid Film and Video), there are three primary ways of writing a film. A *film treatment* is a detailed prose summary of the action of a proposed film—usually two to twenty pages in length. Often, in the mainstream film industry, the treatment receives approval from a studio or producer even before a complete script is written. A *script* or *shooting script* contains the complete dialogue as well as descriptions of the shots, sets, and sound effects. A *storyboard* looks much like a comic book—a series of drawn frames, one frame per shot, with a description of the action or dialogue written underneath the frame. Photocopies of treaments, scripts, and storyboards of well-known films are available for purchase from a number of sources. (Check the back pages of any national film magazine. We have used Script City, 8033 Sunset Boulevard, Suite 1500, Hollywood, CA 90046, 213-871-0707.) Our students have been fascinated to read the original treatment of *Star Wars*, the script to *E.T.*, and the storyboard for *Blade Runner*.

Students have enjoyed writing treatments of a prequel or sequel to a film they have studied in class, for example:

1. Write a treatment of a prequel to *Stagecoach* that focuses on the incident that prompts the Ringo Kid to take revenge on Luke Plummer.

2. Write a treatment of a sequel to *Empire of the Sun* that describes Jamie's life ten years after the war.

Another assignment would be to write a script of a scene from a sequel or a prequel to a film students have watched.

1. Write a shooting script of a scene in a prequel to the film *Ordinary People*. For example, one scene might be of the Jarrett family at dinner before the boating accident.

2. Write a script of a scene in a sequel to *Sugar Cane Alley*. Imagine that José is now an adult with a university education. Is he still living on Martinique? Show a scene from his life. The scene should demonstrate the ways in which his childhood has affected his adult life.

Other assignments ask students to imagine a scene that was alluded to in the film, but was not shown in the film, and to write a shooting script of the missing scene using dialogue and camera directions:

1. In the film *Boyz N the Hood*, the viewer sees scenes from Tre's life when he is about twelve and from the time when he is an older teenager, and is left to imagine what has happened to him in those intervening years. Write a shooting script that shows one of Tre's experiences when he is in the ninth grade.

2. Write a shooting script for a scene for *The Searchers* that depicts an episode in Debbie's life during the years she lives with the Indians.

Finally, some of the more visually oriented students enjoy drawing and writing a storyboard for a proposed scene from a film. Again, they could compose a "missing scene" from a film they have seen in class or from a potential prequel or sequel. Another assignment could have them select a work of literature such as *The Iliad* or Kafka's *Metamorphosis* and storyboard the opening scene of the film.

Bibliography for Chapter Three

Atwell, N. 1987. *In the Middle*. Portsmouth, NH: Boynton/Cook.

Films Cited in Chapter Three

Information provided for each film is title, director, year of release, MPAA rating, and length.

Au Revoir les Enfants, Louis Malle, 1987, PG, 104 min.

Basic Film Terms: A Visual Dictionary, Sheldon Renan, 1970, NR, 14 min. (available from Pyramid Film and Video, 800-421-2304)

Blade Runner, Ridley Scott, 1982, R, 122 min.

Boyz N the Hood, John Singleton, 1991, R, 112 min.

Citizen Kane, Orson Welles, 1941, NR, 119 min.

Empire of the Sun, Steven Spielberg, 1987, PG, 153 min.

E.T.: The Extraterrestrial, Steven Spielberg, 1982, PG, 115 min.

Gallipoli, Peter Weir, 1981, PG, 111 min.

High Noon, Fred Zinnemann, 1952, NR, 85 min.

Hope and Glory, John Boorman, 1987, PG-13, 97 min.

The Maltese Falcon, John Huston, 1941, NR, 101 min.

Musashi Miyamoto (Samurai I), Hiroshi Inagaki, 1955, NR, 92 min.

My Brilliant Career, Gillian Armstrong, 1979, G, 101 min.

Ordinary People, Robert Redford, 1980, R, 124 min.

Pathfinder, Nils Gaup, 1987, NR, 88 min.

Rebel Without a Cause, Nicholas Ray, 1955, NR, 111 min.

The Searchers, John Ford, 1956, NR, 119 min.

Stagecoach, John Ford, 1939, NR, 100 min.

Star Wars, George Lucas, 1977, PG, 121 min.

Sugar Cane Alley, Euzhan Palcy, 1983, PG, 106 min.

A World Apart, Chris Menges, 1988, PG, 114 min.

Chapter Four

Teaching Film Genres

Introduction

When Alan taught a college-level film criticism course in the early 1980s, the course was organized around two major approaches to film criticism: genre criticism (the analysis of groups of popular films from the heyday of the Hollywood studio system) and the *auteur* approach (the analysis of the films of a single director). After we developed ways of teaching individual films in English classes, the next logical step was to teach films in groups, and it seemed to us that the most interesting grouping for students would be by traditional film genres such as the western and the detective film. Although we feared student resistance (the classic genre films date from the 1930s, 1940s, and 1950s, and many are in black and white), the students continued to surprise us with their ability to set aside their prejudices, to engage with these films, and to analyze them with a fair degree of sophistication. Again, the success of the genre units came from revealing to students concepts with which they had had considerable experience, but about which they had not done much thinking, talking, or writing. For example, they knew tacitly about stock scenes or characters in westerns—as evidenced by their ability to list them even before they saw any films in class—but they had not reflected on what the treatment of these stock characters in John Ford's *Stagecoach* tells us about the social attitudes of America in the 1930s. The students' enjoyment of these genre films and their success in analyzing them convinced us that studying films by genre was a valuable addition to the curriculum.

Genre study gives us an opportunity to introduce students both to an important approach to film criticism and to a number of classic films they might not otherwise see. Responding to and writing about genre films further sharpen students' viewing and thinking skills, particularly in the area of comparison/contrast analysis. Perhaps most significantly, genre study has students work with popular movies—an enjoyable activity—and prompts them to see artistry in films they have previously seen only as entertainment.

What Is a Film Genre?

Louis Giannetti defines a film genre as "a recognizable type of movie, characterized by certain preestablished conventions" (p. 444). These conventions are in "style, subject matter, and values" (p. 322); but, Giannetti reminds us, "a genre is a loose set of expectations . . . not a divine injunction. That is, each example of a given story type is related to its predecessors, but not in ironclad bondage" (p. 323). Many film historians and critics point out that genres have arisen out of the financial realities of the film industry: studios make the films audiences want to see, so when a particular type of film is popular, the studios make more of them. When a genre ceases to be profitable, the studios move on to other types. Therefore, genre movies are closely tied to audience expectations developed over dozens, even hundreds, of movies. (See the discussion of this point in Schatz [pp. 3–13], and in Bordwell and Thompson [p. 81].)

For most of the twentieth century, commercial film production has been dominated by genre films. Certainly this is true of the classic Hollywood movies of the period between the advent of sound in the late 1920s through the breakup of the studio system in the 1960s. Schatz reports that, in 1950, ninety percent of all movies released in the United States fell into some preestablished classification, and that four genres together accounted for sixty percent of the films: westerns, crime/detective, romantic comedies, and musicals (p. 6). For evidence that the dominance of genre films continues well into the 1990s, consult today's local listings in your newspaper and note how many you can count on to have predictable plot elements. Recent genre films have included examples of the western (*Unforgiven, The Quick and the Dead, Tombstone, Wyatt Earp*), detective (*Devil in a Blue Dress, Seven*), gangster (*The Godfather, Part III, Natural Born Killers*), international spy/terrorist thriller (*Clear and Present Danger, Rising Sun*), romantic comedy (*When Harry Met Sally, Sleepless in Seattle, While You Were Sleeping*), and horror films (*Mary Shelley's Frankenstein, Interview with the Vampire*). In addition to these films that are clearly members of classic film genres, some interesting new groups of films are developing that may or may not show up later as film genres. For example, there have been a num-

ber of films about body switching (*Big, 18 Again!, Switch*) and gender
crossing (*Tootsie, Mrs. Doubtfire,* and *To Wong Foo, Thanks for Everything,
Julie Newmar*). The teen comedy has produced *Ferris Bueller's Day Off,
Porky's, Fast Times at Ridgemont High, Clueless,* and *House Party* among
many others. We've found that students are quite savvy about these
developing genres when we ask them, "What are the types of movies
that are most popular today?" When we ask them to articulate further
how these movies are alike, they refer to a set of expectations they
have about such movies.

Genre Characteristics

There is no one, universally agreed-upon set of characteristics for analyzing genre films. Bordwell and Thompson offer a list that includes
subject matter, objects, settings, style of performance, and plot pattern
(p. 81). Schatz says, "Simply stated, a genre film . . . involves familiar,
essentially one-dimensional characters acting out a predictable story
pattern within a familiar setting" (p. 6). Schatz goes on to compare the
relationship of the qualities of an individual film to the genre type as
one of "surface structure" to "deep structure" (p. 9). That is, when we
analyze a particular film ("surface structure"), we may take into account a number of "deep structures," such as the political issues of the
day, the industry's financial concerns, or the director's personal touch,
but perhaps the deepest structure of all is the almost mythic requirements of the genre itself.

We have found it useful to analyze genre films with a set of six
characteristics: setting, characters, plot (both typical conflicts and typical structures), iconography (visual images that appear throughout
the history of a genre), mood, and cinematic style. Later in this chapter we describe how these characteristics show up in the genres we've
used most often in English classes.

Film genre study is unlike literary genre study, which generally
focuses only on the structural characteristics of literature. Someone
using a "genre approach" to literature is usually assumed to have organized a course by teaching units on short stories, plays, epics, lyric
poetry, or novels. Genre fiction—such as the westerns of Zane Grey or
the detective mysteries of Raymond Chandler—doesn't show up in
the typical middle or high school literary canon. As with literature,
genre films are often considered less important than non-genre films.
Schatz's distinction between genre films and non-genre films provides
a clue to the different status of both genre fiction and genre films:

> [N]on-genre films generally trace the personal and psychological
> development of a "central character" or protagonist. The central

characters are not familiar types whom we've seen before in movies (like the gangster, the music man, the Westerner). Rather, they are unique individuals whom we relate to less in terms of previous filmic experience than in terms of our own "real-world" experiences. The plot in non-genre films does not progress through conventional conflicts toward a predictable resolution (as with the gangster dead in the gutter, the climactic musical show). Instead it develops a *linear* plot in which the various events are linked in a chronological chain and organized by the central character's own perceptual viewpoint. The plot resolution generally occurs when the significance of the protagonist's experiences—of the "plot line"—becomes apparent to that character or to the audience, or to both.

—T. Schatz (p. 7)

Because genre films are more predictable, familiar, and patterned rather than surprising, individualistic, and unique, they are often dismissed as entertainment rather than praised as art. Therefore, when teachers decide to include film genre study in the curriculum, they first run the risk of being accused of studying inferior works. Moreover, teachers have to shift their critical emphasis from the analysis and evaluation of one individual work to consideration of the work as a part of a large group of works over time.

Key Concepts in Genre Study

We have found that, regardless of the genre, there are four key concepts that inform our study of a group of genre films: formula and novelty, contemporary relevance, psychological appeal, and the stages of genre development.

Formula and novelty. The first issue we explore is how a particular film both conforms to the characteristics of the genre and how it plays out variations on the formula. As Schatz points out in his first chapter, any new western would have to satisfy enough of the audience's expectations to be recognizable as a western; yet, to make money, it would also have to have enough novelty to merit attention. The inevitable result is that any good genre film creates a tension with the formula—similar without being too clichéd, different without violating expectations.

Contemporary relevance. The second key concept in genre study arises from the assumption that genres persist because they provide a way for the filmmakers and audience to explore contemporary events and attitudes through the filter of stories that are distant in time and place (as with the western) or displaced into a familiar plot structure (as with detective films). The question we often ask with a genre film is: What does this film tell us about the time and place of the making of the film? For example, several westerns such as *Broken Arrow* (1950) and *The Searchers* (1956) addressed the topic of racial prejudice—but displaced from the civil rights era to the relative safety of the Old West. *Soldier Blue*, a 1970 western about an Indian massacre, explored issues related to the My Lai massacre, and it did so a full decade before mainstream movies began to deal explicitly with the Vietnam War. *Chinatown* (1974) portrayed a detective revealing corruption in Los Angeles' Water and Power Department of the 1930s for an audience that was immersed in the corruption of the Watergate scandal. As Giannetti states, "The stylized conventions and archetypal story patterns of genres encourage viewers to participate ritualistically in the basic beliefs, fears, and anxieties of their age" (p. 326).

Psychological appeal. A third concept in genre study explores the question, "Why do people want to see so many examples of a particular genre of films?" Schatz suggests that genres explore underlying themes and cultural conflicts that are themselves essentially "unsolvable, irreconcilable" (p. 31). Each film presents a resolution to the particular conflict within the film, but since the cultural conflict persists, the genre continues to explore the theme. For instance, westerns often explore the conflict between individual freedom and civilized social order, so we might expect westerns to surface when issues of individual freedom are of interest to large numbers of people. Similarly, some genres appeal more to men than to women, and vice versa. What is the basis of this division of interest? Beyond social groups or gender, are there individual preferences for particular genres? Are some people drawn to a genre because of an individual search for meaning? We explore questions like these by having our students reflect on their own interest in various film genres and by having them discuss why some people might like one genre more than another.

Stages of genre development. The fourth concept we explore with genre films is how the genre develops over time. Giannetti characterizes four stages in the development of a genre: the *primitive* period, the first appearance of films of a particular kind during which the conventions are established; the *classical* period, during which the genre develops a large following and consolidates the basic values associated with the genre; the *revisionist* period, during which the films are more complex and ambiguous, and the filmmakers begin to question the values inherent in the genre; and the *parodic* period, during which the conventions of the genre are mocked (pp. 326–328). With westerns, this progression is exemplified by Edwin S. Porter's *The Great Train*

Robbery (1903), John Ford's *Stagecoach* (1939), Sam Peckinpah's *The Wild Bunch* (1969), and Mel Brooks' *Blazing Saddles* (1974).

Teaching a Film Genre Unit: The Western

Our experience with teaching film genres to high school students has been largely with the western and the detective genres. We work with these genres because of the large number of films available for each genre and because the classic films in each genre are both appealing to high school students and teachable. Each genre, moreover, has been popular in the 1990s, and our students are familiar with modern western and detective films.

The structure we use for the genre unit works with teaching any genre. We explain here in specific detail how we teach the western. Later in this chapter we will provide the particulars for teaching other genres.

When we teach the western, the introductory lesson consists of a mini lecture, followed by a small group or jigsaw activity. We begin by defining a film genre as a large group of films that share certain characteristics. Then we explain that we will be working with the western genre and in our mini lecture we give the students the characteristics shared by western films: setting, characters, plot, iconography, mood, and cinematic style.

We begin by handing out the chart in Figure 4–1. This chart contains a series of questions that could be asked about any genre.

We have students fill in "Western" at the top of the second column. What happens next can be whole class brainstorming, individual brainstorming followed by discussion, or a jigsaw activity. If we are using a jigsaw activity, we divide the class into six expert groups and give each group one of the characteristics and the defining questions for that characteristic. In part two of the activity, students return to their home groups and teach each of their groups about the characteristic in which they have just become experts. Once the class has determined and described typical characteristics of the western, we show them a chart we have constructed describing the characteristics (Figure 4–2); if necessary, we add characteristics they have come up with that are not on the chart.

We have found it effective to use the following characteristics of a western.

Setting: Classic westerns are set in the American West in frontier towns, on ranches or farms, or on the prairie between the years 1860 and 1910.

Figure 4–1

Typical Genre Characteristics

Genre Aspects	Genre: _____
Setting • Where and when does the typical film take place? • What visual images are associated with the typical setting?	
Characters • Describe the typical heroes or protagonists. • What types of supporting characters would you expect to find? • What roles do men typically have in these films? Women?	
Plot • What are the conflicts you would expect to find in this genre? • Describe typical plot structures in this genre (for example, journey, double mustery, or rise and fall of a character).	
Iconography • What objects or images do you expect to see in a film of this genre?	
Mood • Is the typical film optimistic or pessimistic? Light or dark? Zany or significant? Eerie or wholesome?	
Cinematic Style • What are typical shots, camera movements, lighting, editing techniques, or use of sound?	

Figure 4–2

The Western

Typical Aspects of the Western	Film:
Setting • American West between 1860-1910.	
Characters • Cowboy hero is "strong,silent type"--moral--rugged individualist. • Women are of two types--the "pure" or the "fallen." • Supporting figures may include drunks, sheriffs, codgers, gamblers, dancehall girls, sidekicks, a "doc," and a "good Indian." • Villains are often Indians (viewed stereotypically) or renegade bad men motivated by greed or sheer meanness.	
Plot • Plots often include stagecoach journey, revenge/retribution, cavalry against the savage Indians, bank or stage robberies, face-to-face gunfights. • Conflicts include frontier vs. civilization, freedom vs. conformity, or individual vs. society.	
Iconography • Horses, guns, the land, saloons with swinging doors, tumbleweed.	
Mood • Generally optimistic--the good guys usually win and the bad are usually punished.	
Cinematic Style • Long shots of landscape, mountains, and the horizon; characters placed in context of the frontier. • Shot mainly in daylight.	

Characters: The hero of the western is a cowboy who is moral and a rugged individualist—the "strong, silent" type. Women are one of two types—the "pure" (the rancher's daughter or wife) or the "fallen" (prostitutes, madams). Supporting figures may include drunks, sheriffs, codgers, gamblers, dance hall girls, sidekicks, a "doc," and a "good Indian." Villains are often Indians (viewed stereotypically) or renegade bad men motivated by greed or sheer meanness.

Plot: The characters often undertake a journey on a stagecoach, on a cattle drive, or in a wagon train through unknown—and often hostile—territory. Other plot lines involve revenge or retribution, cavalry against the savage Indians, bank or stage robberies, or face-to-face gunfights. Typical conflicts include frontier vs. civilization, freedom vs. conformity, or individual vs. society.

Iconography: Prominent props include horses, guns, the land, swinging saloon doors, and tumbleweeds.

Mood: The mood of westerns is generally optimistic—the good guys usually win and the bad are usually punished. Sometimes the films are poignant and nostalgic—expressing sadness over the closing of the frontier or longing for simpler times. The western typically affirms American values of individualism and freedom—the right to do what's right without restraint from corrupting society.

Cinematic Style: Long shots of the landscape, mountains, and horizon predominate. Typical establishing shots place the characters in the context of the frontier. The western is a "light" genre, shot mainly in the daylight.

After the students' brainstorming, we point out any details they may have missed. For example, sometimes students do not come up with types of women who appear in westerns. They may not understand that the dance hall girls of classic westerns are actually "fallen" women or prostitutes. This fact is understood by adults who grew up with westerns, but television has sanitized the genre to such an extent that today's students often miss the implications completely.

Sometimes students need to know more about conflicts and plot structures of westerns. When necessary, we point out that typical conflicts include individual freedom vs. civilization, rule of law vs. lawlessness, and settlers vs. Indians. We explain that the structure of the plot is often rooted in a journey or based on the theme of revenge, culminating in a gunfight.

At this point, we sometimes show clips from a variety of westerns to illustrate the characteristics. To illustrate setting, it is usually sufficient to show the first two minutes or so of any western. When we talk about typical characters, we often use a clip from *Stagecoach* (beginning at [0:25:30]) that shows us all of the main characters and especially allows us to note differences between Dallas (the prostitute) and Mrs. Mallory (the aristocratic mother-to-be). We compare this with a scene from *High Noon* (beginning at [0:55:10]), which shows a confrontation between Amy Kane, played by the very blonde Grace Kelly, and Helen Ramirez, played by the Mexican-American actress Katy Jurado. For plot conflicts, the first twelve minutes of *The Searchers* and the opening scene of *Shane* ([0:01:20] to [0:08:30]) work well. For iconography we've used the opening five minutes from *A Fistful of Dollars* and asked students to jot down any objects or images that convey to the viewer "this is a western." In the area of cinematic style, the type of scene that works best is one that situates the characters in a typical western landscape. These usually emphasize horizontal compositions and wide open spaces. The heroes and villains are often shown from low angles, conveying either heroism or threat. A scene in *Stagecoach* (beginning at [1:09:32], depicting the chase and fight between the Indians and the stagecoach) is a good one for demonstrating the style of western action scenes.

Once we have established the characteristics of a typical western, we then show an entire classic film in the western genre—usually John Ford's *Stagecoach*. *Stagecoach* works particularly well with students, perhaps because of its variety of characters and its plot structure. In this film, eight characters—including an alcoholic doctor, a prostitute, the wife of a cavalry officer, a whiskey drummer, a banker, a marshal, a gambler, and an outlaw who has just broken out of prison—make a stagecoach journey from a civilized town through hostile Apache territory to Lordsburg on the edge of the uncivilized frontier. The drama of the journey is heightened by the birth of a baby and the attack by Apaches led by Geronimo.

As students watch *Stagecoach*, they use the chart in Figure 4–2 to make notes on how the film conforms to or departs from the genre. We stop from time to time to check in with the students' progress in comparing and contrasting *Stagecoach* with the typical western. After about twenty minutes of the movie we have met all the characters, so we pause to allow the students to point out character types: John Wayne's Ringo Kid, the strong, silent loner who wants revenge for the death of his brother and who longs to get away from the problems brought about by encroaching civilization; Dallas, the fallen woman with a good heart; Mrs. Mallory, the pure, cultured wife and mother-to-be; Curly, the marshal; the drunken Doc Boone; and Mr. Hatfield, the Southern gambler. During other breaks in the film, students notice the setting: the Arizona territory in the post–Civil War era. We discuss with them the conflicts in the film: revenge, civilization vs. frontier, and soldiers vs. Indians. We look at the plot structure—the stagecoach journey through perilous territory. We make a list of the objects and images—iconography—that appear in the film: black hats, white hats, guns, horses, arrows, wagons, and saloons with swinging doors. At the end of *Stagecoach*, we consider the mood of the film and students generally conclude that the tone of the film is optimistic: Ringo and Dallas go off together to Ringo's ranch—they escape the problems of civilization.

Before we leave *Stagecoach*, we ask the students to look again at the characteristics of films in the western genre and to decide what gives *Stagecoach* its individuality and makes this film different from other westerns. What we hope will emerge are insights into the characters of the Ringo Kid and of the banker, Mr. Gatewood. Ironically, in *Stagecoach*, the presumably upstanding banker is an outlaw, while an outlaw, the Ringo Kid, is the hero. Even though Ringo seeks vengeance, his is the voice of compassion, fairness, and order.

By now the students have a good grasp of the characteristics of the genre and they have analyzed one film using these characteristics. To illustrate to our students how universal these characteristics are, we show them a second western—usually *High Noon*—and ask them to compare this film with both *Stagecoach* and with the typical western characteristics. *High Noon* is a good film to use both because of its unusual structure of unfolding in real time and because of its strong characters. The film begins at 10:45 A.M. on a Sunday morning in Hadleyville. Marshal Will Kane has just married a Quaker woman, Amy, and is handing in his badge and gun when word comes that Frank Miller, a man Kane had arrested, has been released from prison and is arriving in town on the noon train. The arrival of Miller threatens the town with lawlessness, but the people of Hadleyville refuse to help Kane in his fight against the Miller gang. By the time the train arrives, Kane is the sole defender of the town. Kane's character is particularly interesting as is the character of Amy Kane, the wife who hates guns and who walks away from her new husband when he decides to put on his gun to fight Frank Miller. Another strong character is Helen Ramirez, the saloon owner and Kane's former lover, who teaches his new wife about loyalty.

As with *Stagecoach*, we provide a chart for note-taking. In *High Noon*, students again notice typical western characteristics. The characters are typical: the hero is a loner who stands up against the Miller gang as well as against many of the citizens of his town, the film has both a pure woman (Amy Kane) and a fallen woman (Helen Ramirez), and the supporting characters include outlaws, a deputy, and a town drunk. The setting is the American West sometime in the late 1800s. Students also point out the conflicts: revenge and rule of law vs. lawlessness. They notice that the film is based in real time—that the eighty-five minutes of the film are also the eighty-five minutes it takes for the noon train to bring Frank Miller to Hadleyville to exact his revenge. They discuss the film's iconography: the prevalence of horses, guns, badges, clocks, train tracks, and saloons. Students frequently conclude that the film's tone is optimistic because the marshal kills the members of the Miller gang, saves the town, and rides off into the sunset with his bride.

Here, too, we ask students to consider what gives *High Noon* its individuality as a western. They usually point out that the setting departs from that of a typical film of the genre: the location here is not the frontier, but a town with a church and other established institutions. The question in *High Noon* is whether or not the civilized nature of the town can survive if the Miller gang takes over. Students also notice a difference in the plot: a typical western has a lawman in conflict with outlaws. The conflict in *High Noon* pits Marshal Kane against both the Miller gang and the apathy of the town. Although they have decided that the mood of the film is basically optimistic, students also detect a note of bitterness, because Kane throws his marshal's badge on the ground. They interpret this as signaling his disappointment or disgust with the lack of support the town has shown him. The good news is that order is restored and the threat eliminated; the bad news is that the townspeople don't deserve to have what Kane has fought so hard to protect.

Follow-up Topics for Discussion of the Western

Considering formula and novelty. By now students have watched two films in the western genre, so we ask them to compare and contrast these two films—as westerns—either through large or small group discussion. We are particularly interested in their noticing the ways in which the films are different from each other and from typical films in the genre. We hope they will notice the differences in the settings of the two films: the uncivilized nature of the West depicted in *Stagecoach* contrasted with the civilized town of Hadleyville in *High Noon*. The characters are more similar: both Ringo and Will Kane stand alone against an outlaw gang; Dallas and Mrs. Mallory—the fallen and "good" women—are comparable to Helen Ramirez and Amy Kane. Other discussion topics could include the contrast in the narrative structure of each film and a comparison of the mood of the two films.

Contemporary concerns. Another issue we address is what the two films teach us about the time in which they were made. We look at *Stagecoach* and determine what that film shows about American society of the late 1930s. Some students may notice that a villain of the film is the banker—a representative of the business community. The choice of this character as a "bad guy" reflects the feeling toward big business in the Depression Era. Students also point out the sensitivity to a character's social class and race. Dallas, the prostitute, is shunned by Mrs. Mallory, the Virginia-born daughter of a colonel in the Confederate army. The Native American wife of the cantina owner steals the extra horses and runs back to her tribe. Discussion might bring out the fact that the members of the higher social classes were relatively untouched by the horrors of the Depression and set themselves apart from and looked down on the rest of the population of the 1930s.

An examination of *High Noon* in the context of the early 1950s shows a man standing up for his beliefs against everyone in his community. At the same time, a few Americans—including the director of *High Noon*—were standing alone against the intolerance of the House Un-American Activities Committee. Much of the conflict in the film comes from the members of the community being unwilling to take a stand against a threat to the social order of the town. In the 1950s, men and women who took a stand against McCarthyism found themselves alone and ostracized. Blacklisting was particularly harmful to the careers of filmmakers.

The psychological appeal of the western. Another topic for discussion or writing is the enduring appeal of the western. We ask students why westerns continue to be so popular. The appeal may lie in the fact that the films depict simpler times when issues were more clear cut and people knew who the good and bad guys were. Another appeal may be the fact that westerns are quintessentially American, from the wide frontiers to the heroes who carved lives out of often-hostile terrain. From the discussion may emerge the opinion that the appeal lies in the hero, who is usually a good man who defeats evil— something everyone wants to see.

The development of the western genre. "The Western" episode of *American Cinema* (The Annenberg/CPB Collection, Volume 3) provides an excellent history of the genre. We recommend using this documentary after the students have had experience viewing and discussing westerns on their own. Other options for studying the development of the genre are included in the extension activities described on the following pages.

Extension Activities for the Western Genre

1. Have the students examine Gene Autry's "Cowboy Code:"

    1. A cowboy must never shoot first, hit a smaller man, or take unfair advantage.
    2. He must never go back on his word or a trust confided in him.
    3. He must always tell the truth.
    4. He must be gentle with children, the elderly, and animals.
    5. He must not advocate or possess racially or religiously intolerant ideas.
    6. He must help people in distress.
    7. He must be a good worker.
    8. He must keep himself clean in thought, speech, action, and personal habits.
    9. He must respect women, his parents, and his nation's laws.
    10. The cowboy is a patriot. (p. 11)

    —D. Rothel

    In a discussion ask students to characterize *Stagecoach*'s Ringo or *High Noon*'s Will Kane as a cowboy based on Gene Autry's definition. A further activity could ask students to apply Autry's characteristics to our contemporary heroes and decide if these are still qualities our society looks for in its heroes.

2. Explore the development of the western genre. Using the general directions for the comparison essay at the end of this chapter, have the students write an essay in one of the following categories.

    a. Choose another classic western and compare it to the two films shown in class. Suggested films: *The Searchers, Shane, Red River, Gunfight at the O.K. Corral, The Man Who Shot Liberty Valance*, and *Pale Rider*.

    b. Choose a revisionist western and demonstrate how the film takes the typical elements of the western genre and revises them or comments on them. Suggested films: *Once Upon a Time in the West, Unforgiven, Dances with Wolves, The Wild Bunch, The Shootist, McCabe and Mrs. Miller, Silverado*, and the so-called "spaghetti westerns" of Sergio Leone (*A Fistful of Dollars, For a Few Dollars More*, and *The Good, The Bad, and The Ugly*).

    c. Choose a parody western and describe how the film makes fun of the characteristics of the typical western. Suggested films: *Blazing Saddles, Cat Ballou*, and *Rustler's Rhapsody*.

3. Other possible writing assignments include:

   a. Watch a movie that is not—on the surface, at least—a western and write an essay that explains why this film is indeed a typical western. Possible films include *Star Wars, Outland, The Road Warrior,* and *Waterworld.*

   b. Take a genre other than the western, define the characteristics of that particular genre using the chart in Figure 4–1, and then write an essay that might be given as a lecture to the class on that genre. Include a list of typical movies and select clips that would illustrate the characteristics of the genre.

   c. Write a film treatment for a new western (classic, revisionist, or parody). Think of a contemporary issue that could be presented in a western and explain how you would explore the issue. For example, what would be the specific setting? What characters would you include? What conflict would be the central focus?

Teaching Other Film Genres

Teaching other film genres proceeds much as we have described the western unit. We have included background, typical characteristics, and suggested activities for three other genres (detective, gangster, and screwball comedy) because of their particular appeal to adolescents, because many classic films are available on video, and because descendants of the genres still occupy our film and television landscape.

The Detective Genre

The detective film has its roots in a literary genre dating back to Edgar Allan Poe's "The Purloined Letter." The British adopted and developed the type, most notably in the Sherlock Holmes tales of Sir Arthur Conan Doyle and the drawing room mysteries of Dame Agatha Christie and others. The hard-boiled detective, however, is uniquely American, and by the late 1930s, stories by such writers as Dashiell Hammett and Raymond Chandler were finding their way into film. These American films, featuring the hard-boiled detective, include *The Maltese Falcon, Murder, My Sweet,* and *The Big Sleep.* In the 1950s and 1960s, the detective genre came to television with drama series such as "Perry Mason," "Peter Gunn," "77 Sunset Strip," and "Mannix."

Typical Characteristics of the Detective Film

Figure 4–3 provides a chart for note taking with detective films.
   Setting: The classic detective film is set in a large American city

(usually San Francisco or Los Angeles) in the 1940s or 1950s. The scenes are often shot at night in streets or dark interiors. One typical setting is the detective's seedy office.

Characters: The main character is a hard-boiled detective, a private investigator or "private eye" who is isolated, self-reliant, streetwise, and moral. He is often a former policeman with deep-rooted idealism buried underneath a cynical façade. He is a good man in a corrupt world. Philip Marlowe and Sam Spade are examples. Female characters include the *femme fatale,* the dangerous woman who is beautiful and seductive. She is also often a love interest of the detective, but is usually deeply implicated in the crime. She can't be trusted. Lauren Bacall in *The Big Sleep* and Claire Trevor in *Murder, My Sweet* are *femmes fatales.* Supporting characters include gangsters, crooks, psychopaths, hired killers, policemen, bartenders, and wisecracking office girls.

Plot: The films usually have a double-mystery structure with an introductory mystery that is solved quickly. However, solving this beginning mystery leads the detective into a darker, more important mystery that the detective pursues because of his own need to know. Often the detective is called off the case but continues to investigate anyway. Because detective films are often told in flashbacks with voice-over narration from the detective's point of view, time order is confused. The storyline is usually complicated; in fact, it has been rumored that neither Raymond Chandler, author of the novel *The Big Sleep*, nor William Faulkner, one of the screenwriters, could identify the killer of one of the minor characters.

Themes: The typical detective film explores the nature of good and evil, and truth. Good and evil are not absolute in these films. Sometimes it is not always clear who the good guys are. In *The Maltese Falcon,* for example, the viewer is not absolutely certain until the end of the film that Sam Spade will do the right thing. The detective in these films searches for truth, but often he does not find it.

Iconography: Guns—especially handguns—are prevalent in detective films. Other objects include telephones and automobiles. Men and women wear hats that often obscure their faces. Images in these films are of city streets and urban violence. Interiors often depict entrapment emphasized by stairs, mirrors, and windows with blinds.

Mood: The mood of detective films is dark, oppressive, and pessimistic. The world of the detective is a corrupt world filled with violent people. The detective himself is cynical.

Cinematic Style: Many detective films employ a visual style that has come to be known as *film noir,* with low-angle shots of interiors, exaggerated angles, and strong vertical and diagonal elements in frame compositions. Most detective films are literally dark, with realistic sources of light, strong shadows, and high contrast between black and white. The

Figure 4–3

The Detective Film

Typical Aspects of the Detective Film	Film:
Setting • American big city--usually San Francisco or Los Angeles--in the 1940s or 1950s. • Scenes often shot at night in streets or dark interiors; detective's seedy office.	
Characters • "Hard-boiled" detective--a private investigator ("private eye")--who is isolated, self-reliant, streetwise, moral. Usually a former policeman. Deep-rooted idealism buried underneath a cynical façade. A good man in a corrupt world • *Femme fatale*--the dangerous woman: beautiful, seductive--often a love interest of the detective--but also deeply implicated in the crime. She can't be trusted. • Others: gangsters, crooks, psychopaths, hired killers, policemen, bartenders, wisecracking office girls, victims.	
Plot • Often a double mystery structure: an introductory mystery that's solved quickly and a darker, more important mystery that the detective pursues because of his own need to know. (He's often called off the case but continues to investigate anyway.) • Often told in flashbacks with voice-over narration (time order confused). • Told from the detective's point of view. • Complicated storyline.	

Figure 4–3, continued

Typical Aspects of the Detective Film	Film:
Iconography • Guns (especially handguns), telephones, and automobiles • Images of city streets, urban violence • Images of entrapment: mirrors, stairs, windows	
Mood • Dark, pessimistic, oppressive, threatening, cynical, corrupt, bleak, violent. • Life is seen as momentary, subjective, changing. Truth is not out there to be found. • America is not a happy place. • Good and evil are not absolute but are ambiguous.	
Cinematic Style • Closed in--low angle shots of interiors--exaggerated angles. • Realistic sources of light but strong shadows--high contrast black and white. • Verticals and diagonals rather than horizontals. • Tight cutting rather than moving camera.	

editing is characterized by tight cutting rather than by a moving camera. For a more complete discussion of *film noir*, teachers may want to view the "Film Noir" episode of *American Cinema* (The Annenberg/CPB Collection, Volume 2), which discusses the style in depth.

Recommended Detective Films for Classroom Use

When we teach the detective film in high school, the films we use most frequently for examples of the genre are *The Maltese Falcon, Murder, My Sweet,* and *Who Framed Roger Rabbit?* Other films to consider are *Laura, The Big Sleep,* or the revisionist detective film *Chinatown.* Parodies of detective films include *Dead Men Don't Wear Plaid, Murder by Death,* or *The Naked Gun: From the Files of Police Squad.*

Clips That Illustrate the Characteristics of the Detective Film

The opening scene of *The Maltese Falcon* is a particularly good one for demonstrating character (the hard-boiled detective, the *femme fatale,* and the wisecracking secretary), setting (the detective's office), mood (bleak, cynical), and cinematic style (low-angle shots, tight cuts, verticals, and diagonals). The opening scene of *Chinatown* also illustrates genre characteristics: character (detective, the dangerous woman), setting (detective's office), iconography (telephones, windows, and blinds), and cinematic style (tight cuts, closed-in shots of interiors). A humorous scene in *Who Framed Roger Rabbit?* (beginning at [0:46:30]) involves the meeting of Jessica Rabbit and detective Eddie Valiant, and neatly parallels the scenes from the earlier movies.

Extension Activities for the Detective Genre

1. Explore the development of the detective genre. Using the general directions for the comparison essay at the end of this chapter, have the students write an essay in one of the following categories:

   a. Choose another classic detective film and compare it to the films shown in class. Suggested films: *D.O.A., The Jagged Edge, Rear Window, Laura, Chinatown,* and *The Lady in the Lake.*

   b. Choose a revisionist detective film and demonstrate how the film takes the typical elements of the detective genre and revises or comments on them. Suggested films: *Who Framed Roger Rabbit?* and Robert Altman's 1973 version of *The Long Goodbye.*

   c. Choose a parody of a detective film and describe how the film makes fun of the characteristics of the typical detective film.

Suggested films: *Dead Men Don't Wear Plaid, Murder by Death, Ace Ventura: Pet Detective, The Naked Gun: From the Files of Police Squad, Naked Gun 2 1/2: The Smell of Fear,* and *Naked Gun 33 1/3: The Final Insult.*

2. Other writing assignments include:

   a. Watch a movie that is not—on the surface, at least—a detective film and write an essay that explains why this film is indeed a typical detective film. Possible films include *Blade Runner, The Conversation,* and *Blow Out.*

   b. Write a film treatment for a new detective film (classic, revisionist, or parody). Think of a contemporary issue that could be presented in a detective film and explain how you would explore the issue. For example, what would be the specific setting? What characters would you include? What conflict would be the central focus?

3. Watch the "Writing and Thinking About Film" episode of *American Cinema,* which illustrates three approaches to the critical analysis of *Scarlet Street,* a classic crime film. Choose a detective film and write an essay that analyzes that film from these three points of view (genre characteristics, psychological study, and visual style).

4. Analyze a series of strips from "Calvin and Hobbes" (Figure 4–4) that depicts Calvin's detective alter ego Tracer Bullet in pursuit of a math solution. How does the cartoonist use the characteristics of the detective genre and the *film noir* style in this series of strips?

The Gangster Genre

From the earliest days of the movies, audiences have been fascinated by stories of gangsters and criminals. Films like D. W. Griffith's *Musketeers of Pig Alley* captured life in squalid, crime-ridden tenements of New York and Chicago. In these tales of ill-gotten gains, the films depicted such contemporary evils as prostitution and narcotics trafficking, giving these movies a lurid, sinful appeal. The classic gangster films appeared soon after the incorporation of sound: *Little Caesar* (1930), *Public Enemy* (1931), and *Scarface* (1931). These films were scandalous in their references to real criminals (*Scarface* unabashedly alluded to details of Al Capone's career), though in the early days actual names weren't used. The genre continued in its popularity through the 1940s, making the move to television in the 1950s (in series like "The Untouchables") and surfacing again in the movies in

Figure 4–4
Using Calvin and Hobbes to Study the Detective Genre.

Calvin and Hobbes   by Bill Watterson

the 1970s and 1980s, when censorship standards relaxed and allowed more graphic depictions of sex and violence. Popular recent gangster films include the remake of *Scarface* (1983), *The Godfather* (1972) and its sequels, and *Goodfellas* (1990).

Jack Shadoian points out that gangster films often explore a basic conflict in America society—America as a land of opportunity, where getting ahead is valued, versus America as a classless democracy. Other themes include our drive for and fear of success, the violent nature of our cities, the disintegration of the family, and the ineffectiveness of the police and politicians to maintain law and order (pp. 5–10).

Typical Characteristics of the Gangster Film

The chart in Figure 4–5 summarizes the characteristics of the gangster film.

Setting: The classic gangster film always takes place in the "mean streets" of urban, twentieth-century America, specifically in the largest cities: New York and Chicago initially, expanding to Miami and Los Angeles over time.

Characters: At the center of the film is the gangster himself, a man of lower class or immigrant roots with ambition and nerve. We see his rise from humble beginnings through the height of his power and on to his downfall, usually due to a flaw in his nature (not unlike the tragic heroes encountered in the literature curriculum). Families are important in gangster films—both blood families and crime organizations sometimes called "families." Usually, the gangster's literal family figures prominently in the film. The father is often absent; but, if present, he is strict and dominating. The mother is loving, saintly, long suffering, and innocent (or forgiving) about the wrongdoing around her. Often there is a sister, sometimes a brother, and almost always a best friend who stands by the gangster until the bitter end. Sometimes there is an older "mentor" gang boss who serves as a surrogate father to the protagonist.

Other than the gangster's mother and sister, most of the women in these films are prostitutes or mistresses—high-class "gun molls" that contrast with the type of woman the gangster would marry if he stayed in his social class and neighborhood. The gangster's typical relation to women is that he uses them and dumps them rather than marries them; in fact, his most intense emotional connections (outside of his mother and sister) are to men.

Other stock characters in a gangster film include a variety of thugs—bodyguards, drivers, bag men, hired assassins—as well as law-

Figure 4–5

The Gangster Film

Typical Aspects of the Gangster Film	Film:
Setting • The "mean streets" of urban, twentieth century America, specifically New York, Chicago, Miami, and Los Angeles.	
Characters • The gangster is a man of lower class or immigrant roots with ambition and nerve. He rises from his humble beginnings to a position of power, but suffers a downfall due to a flaw in his character. • Both blood families and crime organization "families" figure prominently. • Women consist of the gangster's mother, who is loving, saintly, and long-suffering; the gangster's sister; prostitutes and high class "gun molls." • Stock characters include thugs--body guards, drivers, bag men, hired assassins--as well as lawyers, policemen, entertainers, priests, and crusading politicians.	
Plot • The plot follows the rise and fall of the gangster. • Typical conflicts pit the characters against mainstream society and follow the protagonist's attempt to achieve the American Dream. • Subplots involve gaining and keeping territory and winning wars between the crime families. • Themes include: crime may pay in the short run, but there will eventually be retribution; ambition is more often the cause of the gangster's downfall than excellent police work; and crime can be justified in an unjust capitalist system.	

Figure 4–5, continued

Typical Aspects of the Gangster Film	Film:
Iconography • Objects include guns (particularly handguns and machine guns); illegal substances such as alcohol and drugs; cars, paddywagons, and other motor vehicles. • Interiors consist of closed spaces such as hideouts, retreats, and backrooms. • The gangster's possessions are clues to his rise in society. As he gains power and makes more money, he has dressier clothes, classier apartment furnishings, and more lavishly dressed	
Mood • Somber, dangerous, threatening--pessimistic to the point of fatalism. The gangster's rise to power may have a certain energy, even humor to it, but the end is certain: the gangster will die a violent and undignified death.	
Cinematic Style • Photography is dark. Interior shots prevail, giving the films a claustrophobic, trapped quality. • Many classic films have *film noir* stylistics: black and white or monochromatic colors, high and low angle shots, high contrast light and dark shadows; diagonal compositions, images of entrapment (in mirrors and windows, for example).	

yers, policemen (usually ineffectual, corrupt, or brutal—never admirable), entertainers, priests, and crusading politicians.

Plot: The plot of a gangster film follows the rise and fall of the protagonist with almost Shakespearean symmetry. The typical conflicts set the characters against mainstream society. Often, the protagonist seeks to achieve the American Dream of financial success without regard to the legality of the means. Typical subplots involve gaining and keeping territory, winning wars between the crime families, and so forth. Underlying messages include: crime may pay in the short term, but there will eventually be retribution; ambition (or hubris or some other tragic flaw) is more often the cause of the gangster's downfall than excellent police work; and crime can be justified in an unjust capitalist system.

Iconography: Frequently seen objects include guns (particularly handguns and machine guns); illegal substances such as alcohol and drugs; cars, paddy wagons, and other motor vehicles; and closed spaces such as hideouts, retreats, and back rooms. The gangster's possessions, in particular his clothing, often are clues to his rise in society. As he gains more power and makes more money, he has successively dressier clothes, classier apartment furnishings, and more lavishly dressed mistresses.

Mood: The mood of gangster films is somber, dangerous, threatening—pessimistic to the point of fatalism. The gangster's rise to power may have a certain energy, even humor, to it, but the end is certain: the gangster will die a violent and undignified death. Ironically, we experience both the tragedy of the protagonist's downfall (often we are attracted by his rough appeal) and relief that this scourge to society has been eliminated.

Cinematic Style: The photography of gangster films is always dark. Interior shots prevail, giving the films a claustrophobic, trapped quality. Many of the classic gangster films employ *film noir* stylistics: black and white or monochromatic colors, high- and low-angle shots, high-contrast light and dark shadows, diagonal compositions, and images of entrapment (mirrors and windows, for example).

Recommended Gangster Films for Classroom Use

We recommend using at least one of the three undisputed classics of the early 1930s: *Little Caesar, Public Enemy,* or *Scarface.* Gangster films after 1970 are problematic for classroom use due to their usual R ratings and excessive violence, so teachers may want to use extended scenes from films such as *The Godfather* or *The Untouchables* and leave other films to students' out-of-class viewing (with parental permission).

Clips to Illustrate Characteristics of the Gangster Film

The first shot of Howard Hawks's *Scarface* ([0:02:15] to [0:05:34]) provides a wonderful orientation to the genre. This dolly shot, in medium to long range, is an entire scene and shows a typical setting (a restaurant after a wild party), situation (assassination of a top gangster), and iconography (trappings of success and guns). Moreover, the shot is a great example of how these early films suggest violence without actually showing it.

The opening scene of *Little Caesar* ([0:01:40] to [0:05:02]) is an excellent and succinct example of one of the primary themes of gangster films: someone who is at the bottom strives to be at the top and chooses a life of crime to get there. Rico (Edward G. Robinson) and his accomplice talk in a diner after robbing a gas station. Whereas the sidekick fantasizes about life in the Big City, and the material possessions and women that would be available to him, Rico wants to be a successful criminal for one reason, which he repeats over and over: to "be somebody." A scene early in *Scarface* shows Tony Carmonte's interactions with the police ([0:06:50] to [0:13:00]) and provides an opportunity to discuss many of the typical characters in a gangster film (hoodlums, the current boss, the sleazy gang lawyer, tough-talking and violent detectives, and passive accomplices like the barber).

One of the best demonstrations of the role of the family in gangster films is the opening scenes of *Public Enemy*, which portray the childhood of Tom Powers (played as an adult by James Cagney). When Tom and his friends commit their first big crime (beginning at [0:14:00]), one of the young men is killed. At his funeral, the men talk about what a terrible kid he was while the grieving mothers talk about how he was a good kid who fell in with the wrong crowd. Tom's mother is completely oblivious to the fact that her son is the ringleader of the "wrong crowd." A subsequent scene ([0:39:00] to [0:44:07]) further emphasizes the family theme. Tom's brother returns home after World War I to be told that his brother is a criminal, but his mother insists that Tommy has a "political job." By the time of this scene, Tom's clothes indicate that he is obviously moving up in the world. (Incidentally, this scene is followed immediately by the famous scene of Tom pushing a grapefruit in his girlfriend's face.) The gangster's tendency to "trade up" in cars, clothes, and women is illustrated in the scene where Tom meets Gwen ([0:45:00] to [0:48:40]).

For a more recent take on the gangster genre, the opening scene (stopping at [0:15:25]) of *The Godfather* contrasts the family celebration at the wedding of Don Corleone's daughter with the "family business" being conducted in Don Corleone's study. Here we meet virtually all of the characters of the typical gangster film: the head gangster (here at

the height of his power and more resembling a corporate chief executive officer), the involved as well as the respectable family members,
the loyal lawyer, the semicorrupt entertainer, and the naive and faith-
ful women. Students can easily spot the iconography of clothing, cars,
and guns. In terms of cinematic style, there is a clear contrast between
the *film noir* style of the scenes in Don Corleone's study and the colorful, sunny look of the outdoor wedding reception.

Extension Activities for the Gangster Genre

1. Explore the development of the gangster genre. Using the general
   directions for the comparison essay at the end of this chapter, have
   the students write an essay in one of the following categories:

   a. Choose another classic gangster film and compare it to the
   films shown in class. Suggested films: *Little Caesar, Public Enemy, Scarface* (DePalma's 1983 remake), *The Godfather,* and *Once
   Upon a Time in America.*

   b. Choose a revisionist gangster film and demonstrate how the
   film takes the typical elements of the gangster genre and "re-
   vises" or comments on them. Suggested films: *Underworld
   USA, Bonnie and Clyde, Thieves Like Us, Bugsy, Billy Bathgate,
   Prizzi's Honor, The Untouchables, Menace II Society, Bullets Over
   Broadway,* and *The Godfather, Part II.*

   c. Choose a parody of a gangster film and describe how the film
   makes fun of the characteristics of the typical gangster film.
   Suggested films: *Bugsy Malone* (Alan Parker's 1976 musical
   with a cast of children) and *Dick Tracy* (Warren Beatty's 1990
   mixture of both detective and gangster genre elements).

2. Other writing assignments include:

   a. Watch a movie that is not—on the surface, at least—a gangster film and write an essay that explains why this film is indeed a member of the genre. Possible films include *Jesse James*
   and *Key Largo.*

   b. Write a film treatment for a new gangster film (classic, revisionist, or parody). Think of a contemporary issue that could
   be presented in a gangster film and explain how you would
   explore the issue. For example, what areas of the United
   States or of the world are currently experiencing a lot of
   crime? What would your main gangster be like? Which members of his or her family would you include? What flaw would
   bring about the gangster's fall?

The Screwball Comedy

Screwball comedy is the designation given to a genre of films that flourished in the 1930s and 1940s. These madcap comedies about the battle of the sexes are exemplified by *It Happened One Night, My Man Godfrey, Bringing Up Baby, The Philadelphia Story,* and *His Girl Friday.* These films usually explore how love overcomes obstacles, how couples negotiate a relationship, and what constitutes a "good match." In that the woman is dominant or at least equal to the male, the screwball comedy has a more feminist bent than serious love stories of the same period. Although the genre had run its course by the 1950s, occasionally a film self-consciously recreates the key screwball elements such as Peter Bogdanovich's *What's Up, Doc?,* an affectionate pastiche of the genre with Barbra Streisand and Ryan O'Neal as the mismatched couple. The film-within-a-film of Woody Allen's *The Purple Rose of Cairo* is an example of screwball comedy and would constitute a revisionist take on the genre, pointing out the distance between the world portrayed on film and the world of most of the members of the audience. In the mid-1990s, elements of the screwball genre cropped up in *Four Weddings and a Funeral, While You Were Sleeping,* and *Clueless.*

In addition to movies, there are numerous reflections of the screwball comedy in television situation comedies such as "Moonlighting" (combining screwball comedy and detective genres), "Three's Company," "Bosom Buddies," "Cheers" (especially the early years with Sam and Diane), and "The Nanny." Literary precursors of the genre include Shakespeare's *The Taming of the Shrew* and Austen's *Pride and Prejudice.*

Typical Characteristics of the Screwball Comedy

The chart in Figure 4–6 summarizes the characteristics of the screwball comedy genre.

Setting: The classic screwball comedies are set in urban America of the 1930s and 1940s, in the upper-class milieu of socialites, heiresses, and debutantes.

Characters: First of all, the main character is a couple, a man and woman who are initially mismatched—by social class usually, but sometimes they just irritate each other to the point of hostility—and who we know will fall in love and resolve their conflicts by the end of the film. The pairs of lovers in *It Happened One Night, My Man Godfrey,* and *Bringing Up Baby* set the pattern for subsequent films. Usually the woman is of a higher social class than the man, and she is feisty, headstrong, and proud. Claudette Colbert, Carole Lombard, and Katherine

Figure 4–6

Screwball Comedy

Typical Aspects of the Screwball Comedy	Film:
Setting • Urban America of the 1930s and 1940s, in the upperclass world of socialites, heiresses, and debutantes.	
Characters • The main characters are a couple, a man and a woman, who are initially mismatched--by temperament or social class. • The woman is of a higher social class than the man, and she is feisty, headstrong, and proud. • The men are of a lower class or professionals; they're somtimes clever, but often befuddled and clumsy. • Secondary characters include various friends and relatives of the couple, ditsy rich people, servants, and hangers-on.	
Plot • The mismatched lovers meet (usually bumping into each other by accident), continue to be thrown together against their will, have a series of improbable adventures, grow attracted to each other in spite of themselves, survive comic disasters, and end up hapily engaged or married. • Themes usually explore how love overcomes obstacles, how couples negotiate a relationship, and what constitutes a "good match." There is a "feminist" bent because the woman is dominant or at least equal to the male.	

Figure 4–6, continued

Typical Aspects of the Screwball Comedy	Film:
Iconography • Clothing is important both as a sign of social status and as a symbol of gender role. There are usually lots of evening dresses and tuxedos. Sometimes incidents of cross-dressing occur. • Props include party paraphenalia such as champagne glasses, society orchestras, night clubs, and the trappings of the rich.	
Mood • Light, daffy, and joyously optimistic regarding relationships. The couple may fight and struggle, but love conquers all.	
Cinematic Style • The screwball comedy is dominated by sound--particularly the rapid pace of the dialogue.	

Hepburn are the prototypes here. The men are of a lower class or are working professionals with disdain for the idle rich. For example, Clark Gable is an unemployed reporter, William Powell a butler, and Cary Grant a scientist. These men are clever enough, but are sometimes befuddled and clumsy. These two lead characters talk fast, get themselves into zany situations, and often don't know they're funny (Giannetti, p. 324). There are numerous wacky secondary characters: various friends and relatives of the couple, ditsy rich people, servants, and hangers-on.

Plot: The mismatched lovers meet (usually bumping into each other by accident), continue to be thrown together against their will, have a series of improbable adventures, grow attracted to each other in spite of themselves (with the woman usually the first to discover their love), survive comic disasters, and end up happily engaged or married.

Iconography: Clothing is important both as a sign of social status (there are usually lots of tuxedos and evening dresses) and as a symbol of gender role. Many of these comedies have incidents of cross-dressing—for example, Claudette Colbert in Clark Gable's shirt and Cary Grant in Katherine Hepburn's bathrobe. Prominent props and set pieces include party paraphernalia such as champagne glasses, society orchestras, night clubs, and the trappings of the rich. There are often incongruous objects that contribute to the comedy such as the leopard in *Bringing Up Baby* or the four identical bags in *What's Up, Doc?*

Mood: The tone of screwball comedies is light, daffy, and joyously optimistic regarding relationships. The couple may fight and struggle, but love always conquers all.

Cinematic Style: Unlike other genres with characteristic visuals, the cinematic style of a screwball comedy is dominated by sound—particularly the rapid pace of the dialogue.

Recommended Screwball Comedies for Classroom Use

Of the classic screwball comedies, *It Happened One Night* and *Bringing Up Baby* are delightful and accessible. *What's Up Doc?* is a very funny later film with all of the requisite screwball elements. Episodes from television shows such as "Cheers" and "Moonlighting" also contain easily recognizable screwball elements. The "Romantic Comedy" episode of *American Cinema* (The Annenberg/CPB Collection, Volume 2) contains many clips from classic screwball comedies and shows how the genre developed into contemporary romantic comedies.

Clips to Illustrate Characteristics of the Screwball Comedy

To illustrate the mismatched couple of the classic screwball comedy, the scene in which Gable and Colbert meet in *It Happened One Night* (beginning at [0:07:45]) works well. A scene between Hepburn and Grant early in *Bringing Up Baby* (beginning at [0:14:05]) demonstrates the physical comedy and the witty banter that typify the conflicts between the two characters. A parallel scene in *What's Up Doc?* ([0:09:53] to [0:14:15]) shows the comic meeting between Barbra Streisand and Ryan O'Neal.

The first fifteen minutes of *My Man Godfrey* are excellent for having students identify the iconography of the screwball genre as well as for demonstrating the contrast between the frivolous, wealthy world portrayed in the movies and the hardships of the Great Depression. All of the typical characters appear in these scenes as well.

All of these clips illustrate the fast-paced dialogue typical of the genre, but the dialogue between Hepburn and Grant in an early scene of *The Philadelphia Story* ([0:18:20] to [0:23:45]) has a particularly nasty edge.

Extension Activities for the Screwball Comedy Genre

1. Explore the development of the screwball comedy. Using the general directions for the comparison essay at the end of this chapter, have the students write an essay in one of the following categories:

   a. Choose another classic screwball comedy and compare it to the films shown in class. Suggested films: *The Philadelphia Story*, *His Girl Friday*, and *What's Up Doc?*

   b. Choose a more recent screwball comedy from either film or television, decide whether it is a revisionist or parody treatment of classic screwball elements, and analyze how the film uses the typical elements of the genre. Suggested films and television shows: *The Purple Rose of Cairo*, *Four Weddings and a Funeral*, *While You Were Sleeping*, *Clueless*, and episodes of "Cheers," "Moonlighting," or "The Nanny."

2. Other writing assignments include:

   a. Watch either a romantic comedy from the 1950s (for example, one of the Rock Hudson and Doris Day vehicles like *Pillow Talk*) or one of the "beach blanket" movies of the 1960s. Compare and contrast this film with the typical screwball comedy of the 1930s and 1940s.

b. Write a film treatment for a new screwball comedy (classic, revisionist, or parody). Describe a contemporary "unlikely couple." What would be the differences they would have to overcome? What sorts of adventures would you put them through before you allowed them to finally get together?

Writing Focus: Comparison/Contrast Essay

Assignment to the Students

Write an essay in which you identify a film genre and compare and contrast two films as representative of the genre. Though you may use one of the genres studied in class, at least *one* of the two films must be one that we have not seen in class. Write your essay for an audience of filmgoers who are familiar with the conventions of the genre and who have seen several of its classic films.

Prewriting

Select your genre. If you do not choose a genre we've studied in class, your first task will be to define the genre. Describe the characteristics of a typical film of the genre in any of these categories that apply: setting, characters, plot, iconography, mood, and cinematic style.

Select your two films. Make sure your films are comparable—that is, of the same genre, but with enough differences to make an interesting essay. *Psycho* (1960) and *Dressed to Kill* (1980) are, on the surface, both members of the horror genre, but students who have tried to compare these in the past have found too many similarities. They have concluded that DePalma practically copied Hitchcock's film; there weren't enough interesting differences from which to develop a thesis. In the same way, you can choose two movies that are so different that you have trouble finding interesting comparisons: *Hair* and *42nd Street* are both musicals, but the resemblance ends there. Your most important task in this paper is choosing the right films.

Watch the films. As you watch each film, or immediately after you finish, write down some notes about the genre characteristics of the film. Use the categories listed earlier.

Compare the films using a graphic organizer. Draw two intersecting circles. Label each circle with the title of one of your films. In the intersection of the circles, make notes about similarities. In the rest of each circle, make notes about how each one is different—either from

Figure 4–7

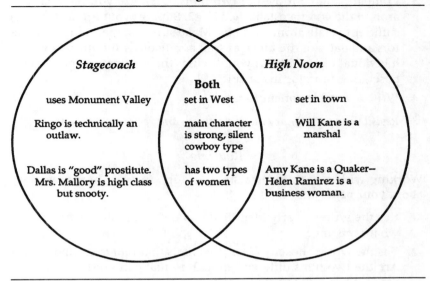

each other or from the typical movie in this genre. Figure 4–7 shows an example of a western comparison.

Drafting

Develop a preliminary thesis statement. Sum up your observations from the comparison exercise in a conclusion. Here are two examples of thesis statements:

1. *Stagecoach* and *High Noon* both contain characteristics of classic westerns, but the two films place different importance on the value of a "civilized" community.

2. As with the typical western, the women in *Stagecoach* and *High Noon* are of two basic types—the pure and the fallen. However, the differences between the women of the two films tell us much about the times in which the movies were made.

Organize your paper. There are many ways you could organize this paper. Use the following outline as a guide.

1. Write an introduction that states your thesis.

2. Write a definition and description of the genre that will form the basis of your comparison. You may identify the typical characteristics of the genre or describe a typical film.

3. Compare and contrast the two films. Organize your comparison around the criteria established in #2. Support your argument with sufficient details from the films. Make sure you mention the directors and dates of the films, as well as any other filmmakers whose individual contributions you discuss (the cinematographer, composer, or editor, for instance).

4. Write a suitable conclusion.

Revisit your preliminary thesis statement and revise it if necessary.

Revising

Working with a partner or a small group, answer these questions about your papers:

1. Has the writer clearly identified and defined a film genre? If not, what's missing?

2. Has the writer chosen at least two films that represent that genre? Are the two films different enough to make interesting comparisons? If not, tell the writer which of the films is not appropriate and why.

3. What is the writer's thesis? Is it clearly stated? If not, what recommendations would you make?

4. Has the writer supported the thesis with sufficient reasons and details? Identify for the writer the strongest and weakest elements of the supporting arguments. Make suggestions about how to improve the weaker arguments.

5. Does the writing have an interesting introduction and conclusion? If not, make suggestions for improvement.

After receiving feedback on your paper from your partner or group, revise your paper in line with their suggestions.

Evaluation

The teacher will evaluate your paper using the following formula:

Definition of genre	20 points
Selection of comparable films	10 points
Thesis	10 points
Supporting evidence	40 points
Introduction and conclusion	10 points
Overall clarity, organization, and style	10 points
Total	100 points

Sample Student Writing About Genres

Students enjoy writing about genre films and succeed in comparing films within a genre (or comparing a film to the genre prototype), and in analyzing the genre characteristics of films that are not obviously a particular genre.

One student compared *Frank and Jesse*, a 1995 made-for-television film, with *Stagecoach*. This excerpt focuses on characters in the two films.

> One other aspect of characters is the women. There is the dedicated wife and mother, and then there are the fallen girls. This aspect fits *Stagecoach* exactly. There was the noble Mrs. Mallory and the fallen Dallas. In *Frank and Jesse* this aspect didn't fit at all. There were several women including Frank and Jesse's mother, Lee, Annie, Ms. Miller, and the bathhouse owner. Frank and Jesse's mother was the typical ranch wife, but the others weren't so easy to categorize. Jesse's wife Lee was a churchgoing woman, but she killed an innocent man. Frank's wife Annie was educated but wasn't the pure type. The bathhouse owner was a rugged woman with good aim. She dressed like a cowboy and acted like a man.
>
> The villains in westerns are usually Indians. This was true in *Stagecoach* but not in *Frank and Jesse*. In that movie, the villains were the James brothers and their sidekicks. The villains in the two movies were similar because they were both driven by meanness and revenge.
>
> —Cessaly Cheatham, Grade 9

Another student compared the recent film *Unforgiven* to the genre type as represented by *High Noon* and *Stagecoach*.

> Over the years, movies have been made to satisfy their viewers' entertainment interests. Such older western genre films as *High Noon* and *Stagecoach* are somewhat different than the westerns being made in the nineties. After watching *Unforgiven*, I became aware of the changing cowboy ways. Although the horses, whiskey, and guns remain the same, the good-natured cowboy role has drastically changed. [Plot summary of film omitted.]
>
> As you can see, like in most westerns, there were the usual townspeople, and those of lower class. However, there was also a no-good marshal (Little Bill), no pure women, of course villains (the bad cowboys), and several people sent to stop the bad guys (William and Kid). Unlike in the typical western genre, I often wondered if anyone was safe from harm. Even though crime was punished, there was a very, very fine line between those who did the punishing and those who should be punished. It is almost as if the good guys were also bad guys.

High Noon and *Stagecoach* both end with a somewhat happy ending. In *Unforgiven*, despite the fact that the goal of the movie was accomplished, and the bad guys handled, the viewers are still left with the feeling that they are back exactly where they started. Of course William was awarded his money which probably helped him financially, but he lowered his standards to meet those of cruel human beings. That is something a good cowboy never does. Therefore, viewers are led to assume that the tone of the entire movie was at times solemn while carrying an overall dark picture.

—Magan Inscoe, Grade 9

Other students analyzed films that are not ostensibly westerns for genre elements. Here are excerpts from two students' essays.

Although definitely not on the surface, the *Star Wars* movies may be the most well-hidden westerns ever made.

The number one trait of a western movie deals with the movie's characters. Typically, there is a hero, his sidekick, a "dame," and a villain. This fits perfectly for this trilogy. Each movie has its hero, Luke Skywalker, a brave young Jedi warrior. His main sidekick is Han Solo, a comical pilot of the Millennium Falcon. Princess Leia, a beautiful Jedi fighter, is the main lady of this film along with the evil villain Darth Vader, who wants control of the world. . . .

About every western there is contains at least one saloon scene. The typical one is filled with drunkards, dance hall girls, a bartender, and a piano player. In *Star Wars* and *Return of the Jedi* there are saloons as well. Although aliens are not cowboys, everything from the typical western is apparent. There are dancing girls, bounty hunters, drinking aliens, gamblers, and even an elephant-like piano player. . . .

As you can see, there are numerous examples of how these movies tie in with those of the western genre. Although not set in the same time frame or place (though some scenes are in the desert), this movie can be directly linked to a western film. Not on the outside, but on the inside, are the *Star Wars* movies true westerns.

—Jared Davis, Grade 9

Some iconography in *Outland* is different than that of typical western films. In this movie, computers and other pieces of high technology equipment can be seen. What remains the same, though, are shots of the entire span of the land. Quite a few shots of Jupiter and Io are shown. This shows how isolated this setting is. Also guns are shown, just like in all western movies. The guns used in *Outland* are a bit more sophisticated though. Other items used in the movie are space suits, swinging doors, and the space station.

Outland generally has the same semi-optimistic tone to it that many western movies possess. My reasoning behind using the prefix *semi-* is because the movie is not the usual happy, good-guys-win type of movie. I consider *Outland* to be more of an "it's-a-hard-job-but-somebody's-gotta-do-it" kind of movie where the good guys still win over bad. Overall still, the mood is the same.

—Hazel Ogugua-Smith, Grade 9

Bibliography for Chapter Four

Bordwell, D., and K. Thompson. 1993. *Film Art: An Introduction.* 4th ed. New York: McGraw-Hill.

Giannetti, L. 1990. *Understanding Movies.* 5th ed. Englewood Cliffs, NJ: Prentice-Hall.

Rothel, D. 1988. *The Gene Autry Book.* Madison, NC: Empire Publishing Co.

Schatz, T. 1981. *Hollywood Genres: Formulas, Filmmaking, and the Studio System.* Philadelphia: Temple University Press.

Seymore, J. W., Ed. 1994. *The Entertainment Weekly Guide to the Greatest Movies Ever Made.* New York: Warner Books.

Shadoian, J. 1977. *Dreams and Dead Ends: The American Gangster/Crime Film.* Cambridge, MA: The MIT Press.

Film Resource for Chapter Four

American Cinema (The Annenberg/CPB Collection, 1994). This was a ten-episode documentary shown on PBS in 1994 and is available on five videocassettes. Especially useful are Volumes 2 ("Romantic Comedy" and *"Film Noir"*) and 3 ("The Western" and "The Combat Film"). There is an additional cassette, available only by mail from Annenberg, with three short segments ("Film Language," "Writing and Thinking About Film," and "Classical Hollywood Style Today"), the first two of which would be effective with secondary students. (The Annenberg/CPB Collection, PO Box 2345, S. Burlington, VT 05407-2345, telephone 800-532-7637)

Films Cited in Chapter Four

Information provided is title, director, date, MPAA rating, and length. Films are arranged alphabetically within each group.

Westerns

Blazing Saddles, Mel Brooks, 1974, R, 90 min.

Broken Arrow, Delmer Daves, 1950, NR, 93 min.

Cat Ballou, Elliot Silverstein, 1965, NR, 96 min.

Dances with Wolves, Kevin Costner, 1990, PG-13, 181 min.

A Fistful of Dollars, Sergio Leone, 1964, R, 101 min.

For a Few Dollars More, Sergio Leone, 1965, PG, 127 min.

Frank and Jesse, Robert Borris, 1995, R, 105 min.

The Good, the Bad, and the Ugly, Sergio Leone, 1967, NR, 161 min.

The Great Train Robbery, Edwin S. Porter, 1903, NR, 10 min.

Gunfight at the O.K. Corral, John Sturges, 1957, NR, 122 min.

High Noon, Fred Zinnemann, 1952, NR, 85 min.

The Man Who Shot Liberty Valance, John Ford, 1962, NR, 123 min.

McCabe and Mrs. Miller, Robert Altman, 1971, R, 121 min.

Once Upon a Time in the West, Sergio Leone, 1968, PG, 165 min.

Outland, Peter Hyams, 1981, R, 109 min.

Pale Rider, Clint Eastwood, 1985, R, 116 min.

The Quick and the Dead, Sam Raimi, 1994, R, 105 min.

Red River, Howard Hawks, 1948, NR, 133 min.

The Road Warrior, George Miller, 1982, R, 95 min.

Rustler's Rhapsody, Hugh Wilson, 1985, PG, 89 min.

The Searchers, John Ford, 1956, NR, 119 min.

Shane, George Stevens, 1953, NR, 117 min.

The Shootist, Don Siegel, 1976, PG, 100 min.

Silverado, Lawrence Kasdan, 1985, PG-13, 132 min.

Soldier Blue, Ralph Nelson, 1970, R, 109 min.

Stagecoach, John Ford, 1939, NR, 100 min.

Tombstone, George P. Cosmatos, 1993, R, 130 min.

Unforgiven, Clint Eastwood, 1992, R, 131 min.

Waterworld, Kevin Reynolds, 1995, PG-13, 136 min.

The Wild Bunch, Sam Peckinpah, 1969, R, 145 min.

Wyatt Earp, Lawrence Kasden, 1994, PG-13, 189 min.

Detective Films

Ace Ventura: Pet Detective, Tom Shadyac, 1993, PG-13, 87 min.

The Big Sleep, Howard Hawks, 1946, NR, 114 min.

Blade Runner, Ridley Scott, 1982, R, 122 min.

Blow Out, Brian DePalma, 1981, R, 108 min.

Chinatown, Roman Polanski, 1974, R, 131 min.

The Conversation, Francis Ford Coppola, 1974, PG, 113 min.

D.O.A., Rudolph Mate, 1949, NR, 83 min.

Dead Men Don't Wear Plaid, Carl Reiner, 1982, PG, 89 min.

Devil in a Blue Dress, Carl Franklin, 1995, R, 101 min.

The Jagged Edge, Richard Marquand, 1985, R, 108 min.

The Lady in the Lake, Robert Montgomery, 1946, NR, 103 min.

Laura, Otto Preminger, 1944, NR, 85 min.

The Long Goodbye, Robert Altman, 1973, R, 112 min.

The Maltese Falcon, John Huston, 1941, NR, 101 min.

Murder by Death, Robert Moore, 1976, PG, 95 min.

Murder, My Sweet, Edward Dmytryk, 1944, NR, 95 min.

Naked Gun: From the Files of Police Squad, David Zucker, 1988, PG-13, 85 min.

Naked Gun 2 1/2: The Smell of Fear, David Zucker, 1991, PG-13, 85 min.

Naked Gun 33 1/3: The Final Insult, Peter Segal, 1994, PG-13, 90 min.

Rear Window, Alfred Hitchcock, 1954, NR, 112 min.

Scarlet Street, Fritz Lang, 1945, NR, 95 min.

Seven, David Fincher, 1995, R, 127 min.

Who Framed Roger Rabbit?, Robert Zemeckis, 1988, PG, 104 min.

Gangster Films

Billy Bathgate, Robert Benton, 1991, R, 107 min.

Bonnie and Clyde, Arthur Penn, 1967, NR, 111 min.

Bugsy, Barry Levinson, 1991, R, 135 min.

Bugsy Malone, Alan Parker, 1976, G, 94 min.

Bullets Over Broadway, Woody Allen, 1995, R, 95 min.

Dick Tracy, Warren Beatty, 1990, PG, 105 min.

The Godfather, Francis Ford Coppola, 1972, R, 171 min.

The Godfather, Part II, Francis Ford Coppola, 1974, R, 200 min.

The Godfather, Part III, Francis Ford Coppola, 1990, R, 170 min.

Goodfellas, Martin Scorsese, 1990, R, 146 min.

Jesse James, Henry King, 1939, NR, 105 min.

Key Largo, John Huston, 1948, NR, 101 min.

Little Caesar, Mervyn LeRoy, 1930, NR, 80 min.

Menace II Society, Allen Hughes and Albert Hughes, 1993, R, 104 min.
Musketeers of Pig Alley, D. W. Griffith, 1912, NR, 12 min.
Natural Born Killers, Oliver Stone, 1994, R, 119 min.
Once Upon a Time in America, Sergio Leone, 1984, R, 225 min.
Prizzi's Honor, John Huston, 1985, R, 130 min.
Public Enemy, William A. Wellman, 1931, NR, 85 min.
Scarface, Howard Hawks, 1931, NR, 93 min.
Scarface, Brian DePalma, 1983, R, 170 min.
Thieves Like Us, Robert Altman, 1974, R, 123 min.
Underworld USA, Samuel Fuller, 1960, NR, 99 min.
The Untouchables, Brian DePalma, 1987, R, 119 min.

Screwball Comedies

Bringing Up Baby, Howard Hawks, 1938, NR, 103 min.
Clueless, Amy Heckerling, 1995, PG-13, 97 min.
Four Weddings and a Funeral, Mike Newell, 1993, R, 118 min.
His Girl Friday, Howard Hawks, 1940, NR, 92 min.
It Happened One Night, Frank Capra, 1934, NR, 105 min.
My Man Godfrey, Gregory La Cava, 1936, NR, 95 min.
The Philadelphia Story, George Cukor, 1940, NR, 112 min.
Pillow Talk, Michael Gordon, 1959, NR, 102 min.
The Purple Rose of Cairo, Woody Allen, 1985, PG, 82 min.
Sleepless in Seattle, Nora Ephron, 1993, PG, 105 min.
What's Up, Doc?, Peter Bogdanovich, 1972, G, 94 min.
When Harry Met Sally, Rob Reiner, 1989, R, 96 min.
While You Were Sleeping, Jon Turteltaub, 1995, PG, 103 min.

Other Films

Big, Penny Marshall, 1988, PG, 98 min.
Clear and Present Danger, Philip Noyce, 1994, PG-13, 141 min.
Dressed to Kill, Brian DePalma, 1980, R, 105 min.
18 Again!, Paul Flaherty, 1988, PG, 100 min.
Fast Times at Ridgemont High, Amy Heckerling, 1982, R, 91 min.
Ferris Bueller's Day Off, John Hughes, 1986, PG-13, 103 min.
42nd Street, Lloyd Bacon, 1933, NR, 89 min.
Hair, Milos Forman, 1979, PG, 122 min.

House Party, Reginald Hudlin, 1990, R, 100 min.

Interview with the Vampire, Neil Jordan, 1994, R, 123 min.

Mary Shelley's Frankenstein, Kenneth Branagh, 1994, R, 123 min.

Mrs. Doubtfire, Chris Columbus, 1993, PG-13, 120 min.

Porky's, Bob Clark, 1982, R, 94 min.

Psycho, Alfred Hitchcock, 1960, NR, 109 min.

Return of the Jedi, Richard Marquand, 1983, PG, 132 min.

Rising Sun, Philip Kaufman, 1993, R, 129 min.

Star Wars, George Lucas, 1977, PG, 121 min.

Switch, Blake Edwards, 1991, R, 104 min.

To Wong Foo, Thanks for Everything, Julie Newmar, Beeban Kidron, 1995, PG-13, 109 min.

Tootsie, Sydney Pollack, 1982, PG, 110 min.

Chapter Five

Film Across the Curriculum

Introduction

We had our first experience in teaching film "across the curriculum" when Ann was called on to design language arts experiences for a seventh-grade interdisciplinary unit on Japan. Ann called Alan: "What can we do with film after I've taught *The Master Puppeteer*?" "Show 'em a samurai film," was Alan's cavalier reply. After all, wasn't that what Japanese cinema was best known for?—at least as far as a thirteen-year-old was likely to care? The only task, it seemed, was a simple one: which samurai film? Eight samurai films later, Ann and Alan chose a film with the unlikely title of *Samurai I* (original title: *Musashi Miyamoto*)—and for the most basic of reasons: it was in color and the color costumes helped our Western eyes keep the individual characters straight. It was, moreover, an exciting film, an appealing story with battle scenes and swordplay, humor and romance.

The only thing we worried about was whether the students would accept the subtitles. We decided to appeal to their pride and address the issue head on. "This film is in Japanese," we told them matter-of-factly. "So that we can understand what they're saying, the distributors have printed the dialogue in white letters at the bottom of the screen." They looked a little dubious. "We'll be stopping every fifteen minutes or so to see if you have any questions. Do your best to get the gist of what they're saying, but don't forget to look at the rest of the screen also." And off we went. The students adjusted quickly to the subtitles and loved the film. When they found out there were two sequels, they begged to see those also. We declined, but we did show them a few scenes from the later two films, so that they knew how the story turned out.

We learned several important lessons with samurais and seventh graders. First, we learned not to be afraid of subtitles, and that realization opened up an amazing array of films to use in the classroom. Second, we learned never to underestimate the caliber of films our students are capable of appreciating. Finally, we learned that students will succeed when teachers prepare them for a viewing experience, support them as they watch the film, and develop interesting follow-up activities.

The theoretical frameworks and strategies we have described in the first four chapters can be applied to a wide variety of films for use in subjects across the curriculum. In this chapter, we begin with a rationale for teaching with and about film in subjects other than English. Next we discuss general strategies for teaching documentaries and other nonfiction films. We then describe specific ways to use film in social studies, science, math, foreign language, and visual and performing arts, and suggest films appropriate for each subject. Considering English as a content area, we make recommendations about the place of film study in the scope and sequence of secondary English/language arts curricula.

Rationale for Teaching Film Across the Curriculum

We advocate using the active viewing strategies described in our first four chapters in subjects beyond the English classroom for three reasons: teachers already use film frequently, but in ways that do not engage students actively; film provides an excellent opportunity for interdisciplinary teaching; and the films used in other curricular areas can be used to develop students' critical viewing skills.

First, teachers in all content areas are already using videos as a part of their curriculum—as a "visual aid" source of content information or as a supplement to a particular unit—but our observation has been that teachers tend to turn on the projector or VCR and let the film do the teaching. At best, the teachers provide a brief introduction before the film and study questions at the conclusion. At worst, teachers use a related film as a break from the routine of note-taking and problem solving or as a filler between the conclusion of a unit and a holiday break. Almost never do the teachers provide students with activities while they are viewing, stop to check for understanding at key points in the film, or have students respond to cinematic techniques used to convey the information.

Content-area teachers use a wide variety of films on video. Often these videos are of the instructional variety—videos that exist solely for classroom use. These videos are the much-improved descendants of films we remember from our own high school days—a historian or scientist or John Cameron Swayze talking directly to the audience and taking us on a journey to a faraway land or "inside Mr. Atom." (How we groaned when the Encyclopedia Britannica logo appeared on the screen.) A second category of these films is documentaries produced for television or other mass distribution—such as PBS' "The Civil War" or "Eyes on the Prize" or the excellent "National Geographic Specials." Finally, teachers often use feature-length fiction films to supplement their curriculum: *Gallipoli* or *Glory* to enrich a history unit, *Jean de Florette* in a French III class, or *Stand and Deliver* to motivate the study of higher mathematics.

Our experience has been that interdisciplinary curriculum development is a growing trend in secondary schools, particularly in middle schools, so a second reason for using film across the curriculum is that film provides great opportunities for integrating content areas.

Our seventh-grade samurai experience is an example of how we used a film as another type of art from the culture being studied. Students had held a tea ceremony, folded origami cranes, painted a screen or fan, eaten sushi, and read a novel set in Japan. Watching a samurai film was another cultural experience—and one in which they could notice many of the aspects of Japanese culture they had learned about in other experiences or from other media.

Another approach to using a film as an opportunity for curriculum integration derives from the nature of filmmaking as a collaborative art: to tell a story a film employs language, costumes, makeup, sets, locations, music, sound effects, dance, color, light, frame composition, and juxtaposition of images. A good historical film, for example, will provide information about the clothing, architecture, food, arts, and culture of a particular period. A contemporary film set in a foreign country will show us the geography of the place (the terrain, housing, food, clothing, occupations, religion, customs, social conditions), let us hear the sounds of the place (the languages, dialects, and music), and portray vividly some of the issues confronting the people who live there.

A third reason for developing effective strategies for using film in the various content areas is to answer the growing call for students to be "media literate." Groups like the Commission on Media of the National Council of Teachers of English continually urge the inclusion of media studies in the K–12 curriculum. For example, in NCTE's 1991 "Report on Trends and Issues," the Commission on Media states:

> [D]efinitions of contemporary "literacy" must recognize that an understanding of visual, as well as verbal, texts is essential in today's world. Therefore, the Commission supports development of media-inclusive language arts curricular models that acknowledge and

build upon the rich variety of ways that our students, and their teachers are influenced by forms and content present in modern communication. . . . Inclusion of the study of media certainly should no longer be optional in our schools. . . . We must send students the message that critical thinking extends beyond print.

—Suhor, p. 2

Language arts educators such as Barchers (1994), Considine and Haley (1992), and Sinatra (1986) suggest that the ability to understand and produce visual images is an essential component of contemporary literacy. Some curriculum frameworks have even included viewing as the "fifth language art" (see, for example, North Carolina's *Competency-Based Curriculum Teacher Handbook, English Language Arts K–12*).

When we consider viewing as a receptive/decoding process akin to reading or listening and visual composition as an expressive/encoding process parallel to writing and speaking, we can advocate the inclusion of critical viewing skills across the curriculum in much the same way that we use content-area reading and writing activities in all subjects.[1]

General Strategies for Teaching Nonfiction Films

If a teacher's primary goal for showing a documentary film is to impart the information contained in the film, the teacher may want to use a note-taking guide like the ones in Figure 5–1, which allow students to take notes about the facts and opinions presented (option 1) or, more generally, to take notes about the content information (option 2).

In either case, we recommend that teachers also ask students to note what they are seeing and hearing, so that in the subsequent discussion, the class can describe the filmmaking techniques used to convey the information and discuss whether the makers of the film are themselves expressing opinions or biases, whether they are openly or subtly persuading the viewer to believe the truths they are presenting.

In order for the visual and auditory analysis of a nonfiction film to be meaningful, the discussion must proceed from knowledge of what constitutes traditional documentary style. Although much has been written about this topic (see for example Giannetti, 1987, pp. 302–331), in general, a realistic style of cinematography—that is, a style that most approximates how we see and hear the world—has the following characteristics:

- The *shots* are more frequently long and medium shots, rather than close-ups, and they are from eye level, rather than from high or low angles.

Figure 5–1

Note-Taking Guides for Non-Fiction Films

Option 1

Film Title:	
Facts Presented	**Opinions Expressed**
Cinematic Elements	
Visuals	**Soundtrack**

Option 2

Film Title:	
Content Information	
Cinematic Elements	
Visuals	**Soundtrack**

- *Camera movement* follows the action, rather than having the action occur within a fixed, carefully composed frame. Filmmakers often use a hand-held camera in documentary work, so the movements are rough rather than smooth. If the subject of the shot is in motion, it may in fact leave the frame at given points. This *cinéma vérité* style of cinematography places the viewer in the middle of the action and gives us a "you-are-there" feeling.

- *Editing* in a documentary is usually by means of cuts; fades, dissolves, and optical effects are used more rarely. The length of shots is determined by the action; but, in general, the takes are longer and the action is captured continuously, rather than in the usual combination of shots from various camera setups.

- *Lighting* is by available light—or at least by a visible source of light (such as lamps or streetlights).

- *Sound effects* are recorded live or at the scene, rather than synthesized and added later.

- *Music* is from a source—such as a radio, phonograph, or juke-box—visible in the film, rather than from an orchestral "under-score."

Students are familiar with this style of cinematography from television newsreel footage (although, usually this footage is accompanied by the reporter's voice-over narration) or from some of the "real-crime" shows like "Cops" and "Rescue 911." They may also recognize that the style is sometimes used in fiction films or television shows like "NYPD Blue" and "ER" in order to provide the necessary realism.

As with the fiction films discussed in Chapters One through Four of this book, students need to understand basic film terminology in order to analyze these films thoroughly. Also, teachers may first practice with clips from several nonfiction films or they may begin directly with a viewing guide for one film. Questions that work with any nonfiction film are:

Visuals

1. What information or characters are presented in a close-up?
2. Which characters or objects are viewed with high- or low-angle shots?
3. Which sequences use a moving or hand-held camera?
4. Describe the editing. Are there many quick shots or jump cuts? Are there sequences with long, uninterrupted shots?

Sounds

1. What are the sources of monologue or dialogue in the film? Is there a voice-over narrator? Interviews? Conversations "captured live?"

2. What sound effects did you notice in the film? To the best of your perception, were they recorded live or added later?

3. What music was used in the film? Did it have a visible source, or was it a composed "underscore" added later? What effect did the music produce in scenes where it was used?

4. Did the filmmakers use music and sound effects to add emotion to a particular sequence?

Overall Effect

1. How do the cinematography and sound affect the message of this film?

2. Does the film present a particular point of view, opinion, or bias? Is that point of view stated directly or is it a conclusion you have drawn after analyzing the filmmaking techniques?

Film in the Content Areas

The remainder of this chapter describes strategies for incorporating films in various content classrooms.

Using Films in Social Studies

Because of its ability to capture the rich details of distant times and places, film is particularly well suited for the study of history and geography. Strategies vary from the close viewing of clips for details about the time or place to using whole films to support the study of an era or region.

Historical films present a dilemma. The richness of detail is seductive (this *must* be exactly how it was), yet we know that each detail of set, costume, and makeup is the re-creation of contemporary artists. Moreover, the necessities of a two-hour plot often result in distortions of the facts in service of a good story. This dilemma is the subject of Mark C. Carnes' *Past Imperfect: History According to the Movies,* a collection of essays by historians. In all, sixty historians choose a historical film or group of films and discuss each film's authenticity. In a magazine article describing the book ("Hollywood History"), Carnes concludes that, in general, the sets and costumes of these films re-create the period authentically, and occasionally the films capture the mood of an era or the significance of major historical events. However, in many cases, the filmmakers are cavalier with the facts, omitting and rearranging events and characters, interpreting events to fit contemporary beliefs and values. Therefore, all historical movies come with a caveat: Don't assume that what you're seeing is the way it was. Carnes concludes that historical films provide a rich occasion for "conversation between the past and present."

> Filmmakers have said much about the past. They have spoken both eloquently and foolishly. Sometimes their fabrications have gone unnoticed, sometimes their truths unappreciated. But they have spoken, nearly always, in ways historians find fascinating.
> —Carnes, "Hollywood History," p. 84

When teachers use films to support the teaching of history, they take on the responsibility for having students understand the degree to which the film accurately represents historians' best thinking about the events portrayed in the movie.

One instructional strategy is to use only selected scenes from a film. For example, Bertolucci filmed parts of *The Last Emperor* in Beijing's Forbidden City. A marvelous sequence at the beginning of the film [0:08:56 to 0:14:50] shows the young Pu Yi arriving at the palace to meet the Dowager Empress for the first time. Teachers could have students pay close attention to the sequence and then recall as many details as possible, particularly details that would give clues as to the cultural values of the Chinese royalty.

Similar scenes that lend themselves to this type of activity are from the following films. (Complete citations are in the filmography at the end of the chapter.)

The Return of Martin Guerre [0:01:35 to 0:05:20]

The wedding of Bertrande and Martin provides an excellent opportunity for students to note details of the setting, costumes, and customs.

The Inner Circle [2:06:30 to 2:13:45]

Documentary footage combines with dramatic re-creation to depict the panic that ensued at Stalin's funeral.

Das Boot [0:13:24 to 0:15:30]

A journalist tours a German submarine, shown primarily in two hand-held shots.

Another effective strategy is to select a scene from a film that depicts a specific historic incident, show the students the clip, and then ask them—first of all—to brainstorm a list of factual incidents portrayed in the movie. Then, have them speculate how they might check these facts to determine if the scene is at all accurate. They might suggest checking these facts by consulting encyclopedias, eyewitness accounts, memoirs, history books, biographies, and so forth. The whole class could investigate this first event together—like a scavenger hunt in the school media center or public library. In a follow-up assignment, ask each student to choose a particular event from a historical film, draw up a list of factual incidents, check as many of the facts as possible, and write a paper evaluating the accuracy of the film portrayal of the incident.

Historic events for group or individual analysis include: the climactic battle scene in *Glory*, the massacre of school children in *A Dry White Season*, the battle of Agincourt in Kenneth Branagh's *Henry V*, Stalin's funeral in *The Inner Circle*, and the assassination of Gandhi in *Gandhi*.

Sometimes teachers wish to use whole films to supplement a social studies unit. We recommend that teachers develop a viewing guide as described in Chapter Three, perhaps adding a section for "Facts to Check," where students could jot down questions about particular details that they find unbelievable or that contradict previous information they've learned in the unit. Teachers may wish to consult *Past Imperfect* to determine if a historian has written about the particular film. In any case, the teacher is responsible for clarifying errors of fact or interpretation.

The following is a list of films recommended for use—in whole or in part—in secondary history classes, arranged by country and historical period. See the filmography at the end of the chapter for full citations.

China
The Last Emperor. Three-year-old Pu Yi is taken from his home and named Emperor of China in 1908. In a film that depicts China as a country in the midst of violent transition, Pu Yi goes from the position of "Lord of 10,000 Years" to that of a poor gardener. Actually filmed in Beijing's Forbidden City, this movie is a vivid chronicle of life in that country in the early twentieth century.

France
Danton. Gerard Depardieu portrays Danton in this challenging film by Polish director Andrzej Wajda, who casts French actors in the roles of the democratic supporters of Danton and Polish actors as the opposing, totalitarian followers of Robespierre. The resulting tension

comments on the situation in Poland in the 1980s as much as on the French Revolution.

The Return of Martin Guerre. In this film based on a famous court case from sixteenth-century France, the unhappily married Martin leaves his wife Bertrande to go to war. When he returns years later, the villagers recognize him and Bertrande takes him back into her home, but the returned Martin is changed, noticeably more attentive and loving. A dispute over property leads some of the villagers to question whether he is in fact the real Martin. The film is noted for its attention to period detail and for the assistance of historian Natalie Zemon Davis in the making of the film.

India

Gandhi. This much-honored biography of Mahatma Gandhi portrays his life from his days as a young lawyer in South Africa through the struggle for the independence of India and his assassination.

A Passage to India. This sweeping adaptation of E. M. Forster's novel captures India at the height of British colonialism, with tensions brewing that will result in India's independence.

Japan

Samurai Trilogy. Individual films in this series are *Musashi Miyamoto, Duel at Ichijoji Temple,* and *Duel at Ganryu Island.* In the first film of the Samurai trilogy, Takezo (later to become the famous samurai Musashi Miyamoto) is young, wild, and foolish. Taken in hand by a Buddhist priest who first teaches him discipline and then the way of the samurai, Takezo begins the training that is to make him one of the most respected men in medieval Japan. The second film follows Miyamoto as he continues to strive for the ideals of the samurai. Now a famous swordsman, Miyamoto is challenged to a duel by a young samurai eager to prove himself. The duel, fought in a rice paddy, is a vivid example of the skill of samurai warriors. In the final film of the trilogy, Miyamoto longs to retire from fighting. Before he can lay down his swords and live a contemplative life, he must fight a duel with the skilled Sasashi on Ganryu Island.

Sanjuro. A samurai comes to the aid of a group of young warriors in this satirical sequel to *Yojimbo.*

The Seven Samurai. Set in sixteenth-century Japan, this epic film tells the story of farmers who hire seven samurai for protection against bandits.

Yojimbo. This film is a samurai version of a classic western plot: The hired warrior comes to a violent town to make peace between the combatants and discovers that both sides harbor unsavory characters.

Latin America
The Official Story. In the turbulence of the 1970s, an Argentinean woman, wife of a highly placed government official, begins to suspect that her adopted daughter's parents were murdered by the government.

Missing. Based on the true story of a writer who disappears during the military coup in Chile, this film focuses on the attempts by the writer's father and wife—who are initially on opposite ends of the political spectrum—to locate him and to make sense of the situation.

El Norte. This film, further annotated in Chapter Nine, tells the story of a brother and sister who travel from their native Guatemala through Mexico to California. The movie vividly contrasts the immigrants' native culture with their new surroundings. The film also provides a human dimension for a discussion of illegal immigration.

North America
The Black Robe. A Jesuit priest journeys through seventeenth-century Ontario to convert the Huron Indians. Violent and disturbing, the film has been praised for its realistic depictions of the Huron culture.

Russia/Soviet Union
Alexander Nevsky. Nevsky was a thirteenth-century Russian hero noted for his defeat of Teutonic invaders in a famous battle on a frozen lake. Eisenstein's design and direction are at his most formal. The close collaboration with composer Sergei Prokofiev results in a remarkable integration of film and music.

Ivan the Terrible, Parts I and II. Considered Eisenstein's masterwork, these two parts of a projected trilogy tell the story of Ivan's reign as czar in sixteenth-century Russia. The film is known for its stunning photography (including some color footage).

Peter the Great. This television miniseries tells the story of the great eighteenth-century Russian czar noted for his "Westernization" of Russia and for founding St. Petersburg in order to provide Russia with a port. Shot on location in the heart of old Russia, the film has some stunning sequences.

The Battleship Potemkin. One of the most important films of the silent era, *Potemkin* showcases Eisenstein's formal approach to cinematography and editing. The film tells the story of a mutiny aboard a battleship in the Black Sea at the onset of the 1905 revolution. Most memorable is the sequence depicting the massacre of innocent Sunday strollers on the Odessa steps, a much-honored and parodied scene.

The Inner Circle. Based on a true story, and with the distinction of being the first Western film shot on location in the Moscow Kremlin, *The Inner Circle* tells the story of Ivan Sanshin, film projectionist for

Joseph Stalin during World War II. The film convincingly portrays the harshness and paranoia of the Stalinist era from the point of view of ordinary citizens. Particularly memorable is the depiction of Stalin's funeral and its attendant pandemonium.

South Africa

Cry Freedom. This biography of black South African leader Steven Biko has been criticized for focusing too heavily on his friendship with white journalist Donald Woods and Woods' escape from South Africa, but the scenes of Biko's arrest and interrogation are powerful.

A Dry White Season. A white Afrikaner schoolteacher becomes aware of the toll of apartheid when his black gardener, an old friend, is murdered. A powerful scene early in the movie graphically depicts soldiers shooting schoolchildren.

The Power of One. This film, further annotated in Chapter Six, tells the story of P. K., an English boy born in South Africa, from his birth in 1930 until he leaves South Africa to go to Oxford in 1948. One issue this film addresses, which is not as clear in other films about South Africa, is the three-way tension between English-speaking whites, Afrikaners, and black South Africans.

Sarafina! (further annotated in Chapter Six) and *A World Apart* (further annotated in Chapter Seven) show apartheid from the point of view of two teenage girls, one black and one white.

United States History

Roots. The six episodes of this television miniseries depict the history of African Americans from the capture of Kunta Kinte in 1767 until Reconstruction. (See Chapter Six for additional annotation of Episode 1.)

Glory. This true story of the 54th Massachusetts Infantry, the first black volunteer unit in the Civil War, has been praised by historians for its accuracy in depicting battle scenes.

The Long Walk Home. A maid in Montgomery, Alabama, supports the 1955 bus boycott by walking nine miles to work. Her affluent employer tries to help by providing transportation to the boycotting workers, thus incurring the wrath of her husband and the town's white establishment. The film received praise for its accurate depiction of the 1950s and for the development of the relationship between the two women.

Malcolm X. Spike Lee's controversial biography of Malcolm X may take some liberties by inventing or combining characters, but there are powerful scenes of Malcolm's life prior to prison, his conversion to Islam, his leadership during the Civil Rights Movement, and his hegira to Mecca—all depicted in Lee's expressionistic cinematic style.

World War I

Gallipoli. In this film, further annotated in Chapter Six, two young Australians' glorious dreams of war become a nightmare of trench warfare and slaughter.

The King of Hearts. In Phillipe De Broca's charming fantasy, set in France near the end of World War I, a young Scottish lieutenant searches throughout a small town for explosives left by retreating Germans. Unbeknown to him, all normal citizens of the town have evacuated, leaving only the inmates of the local asylum, who have assumed roles as leaders of the town.

Legends of the Fall. The events of World War I are not the primary focus of this sprawling family saga set in Montana in the first half of the twentieth century; but, in several scenes early in the film, the father and his three sons debate whether the war "is ours to fight." The youngest son joins up and the second son follows to protect him. There is one vivid battle scene that gives a sense of combat typical of the war.

World War II

Das Boot (The Boat). This German film presents an atypical view of World War II—from the perspective of the German crew of a U-boat patrolling waters off the coast of Europe.

Korczak. Dr. Korczak, a Polish pediatrician, takes loving care of two hundred Jewish orphans who have been herded into the Warsaw ghetto during World War II. This film is the heartwarming story of the doctor, his relationship with the children, and his defiance of their Nazi captors.

The Night of the Shooting Stars. Set in the Italian countryside during one night toward the end of World War II, this film shows the conflict between the villagers who support the fascists and those who welcome the approaching liberators—seen from the point of view of a young girl.

Schindler's List. Steven Spielberg's monumental film version of Thomas Keneally's novel tells the true story of Oscar Schindler, a German manufacturer who employs Jews in his factory and thereby saves them from extermination. Scenes of Nazi atrocities are brutally graphic, but the power of the film is undeniable.

Europa, Europa. This film, further annotated in Chapter Eight, is the true story of Solomon Perel, a Jewish teenager who avoids the concentration camps by passing as Aryan in a training school for elite members of the Hitler Youth.

The Nasty Girl (Das Schreckliche Mädchen). This film, further annotated in Chapter Nine, is another true story. For a high school research project, Sonya Rosenberger writes an essay on "My Hometown During the Third Reich," which offends the town leaders who have successfully obscured their roles during the war.

Using Films in Science and Math

Our observation is that most of the films used in science and math classes are of the instructional/documentary variety, but there are a few feature-length fiction films that are notable for their demonstration of the scientific method within the context of a compelling narrative. One of these films also addresses the importance of statistical accuracy in a scientific experiment.

Never Cry Wolf is an adaptation of the book by Farley Mowat and describes a biologist's attempt to stop the wholesale killing of wolves in the Arctic by proving that they don't subsist primarily on a diet of caribou. To discover what the wolves eat, the scientist sets up a camp and begins to observe the comings and goings of an extended family of wolves. In the process, we learn a tremendous amount about the habits of these wolves. When the scientist notices that the wolves eat field mice, he decides to test the hypothesis that a large mammal could live on a diet of mice, and he does so using himself as a test subject.

Similarly, *Lorenzo's Oil* takes a potentially tedious topic—developing and testing a drug to treat a rare disease—and places it in the context of parents fighting to save the life of their son. Michaela and Augusto Odonte are parents of five-year-old Lorenzo, who has adrenoleukodystrophy (ALD), a rare terminal disease. The Odontes, determined to keep their son alive, battle both the medical establishment and parent support groups, which seem reluctant to work quickly to discover a treatment for the disease. The parents undertake medical research on their own and eventually locate oils that stop ALD's progress. The film shows the parents studying the literature on the disease, testing combinations of various oils on their son, conducting blood tests, and charting the results. The movie has added impact because it is a true story; it concludes with a number of real children testifying to the effect of Lorenzo's oil in their lives.

Apollo 13 is another film that contains a demonstration of the scientific method. This true story of the National Aeronautics and Space Adminstration's (NASA's) troubled mission to the moon in 1970 is suspenseful in spite of the fact that the audience knows the outcome. Will the three astronauts have enough power to return to earth? Will the oxygen last? Can they manually position the capsule for re-entry so that they won't burn alive when they hit the earth's atmosphere? This is a great science film, not so much because of the deeds of the astronauts, but because of the truly heroic efforts of the scientists and engineers back at NASA headquarters, who use their knowledge and ingenuity to invent solutions to problems they never expected to face. In one of the most suspenseful sequences of the film, the astronauts discover that there is too much carbon dioxide in the atmosphere of the lunar module. The earth-bound scientists back at NASA are given the problem: Devise an apparatus that will reduce the carbon dioxide, using only the materials available to the astronauts. After viewing this sequence, students could identify elements of the scientific method as well as the types of analytical and creative thinking the scientists do in order to solve the problem.

With *Never Cry Wolf*, *Lorenzo's Oil*, and *Apollo 13*, we recommend teachers make a viewing guide that includes, in addition to the cinematic elements and some open-ended questions, a box for "Elements of the Scientific Method" or "Stages of the Experiment" in each section of the film.

Math is apparently not as compelling for filmmakers as science. The only movie we've found that deals with math in the lives of adolescents is the excellent *Stand and Deliver*, the true story of Jaime Escalante, a teacher in the east Los Angeles barrio who takes on teaching calculus to his discouraged Hispanic underachievers, with astonishing results. There isn't much actual math in the movie, but there is inspiration and a demonstration of the relevance of academic success in everyone's life.

Using Films in the Visual Arts

Film is, of course, a visual medium, and almost all of the terms used to describe painting, drawing, or still photography can be used to describe particular frames, shots, or sequences of a movie: composition, framing, design, balance, lighting, color, chiaroscuro, symmetry, focal point, perspective, shape (particularly circles, triangles, and quadrilaterals), detail, texture, and line (vertical, horizontal, and oblique).

One of the best activities an art teacher can use is to follow the teaching of terms related to visual composition with having the students view clips from films by directors known for careful frame composition (Welles, Wyler, Antonioni, Fellini, Bergman, Scorsese, Hitchcock—to name a few) and have the students apply the art terms to the design of the film shots. Here are two scenes to start with (complete citations are in the filmography at the end of the chapter).

Akira Kurosawa's Dreams [0:12:40 to 0:24:30]

In a segment titled "The Peach Orchard," a young boy follows a mysterious woman out into the countryside, where he has a vision of magnificent dolls come to life.

The Umbrellas of Cherbourg [0:28:53 to 0:32:11]

Two lovers walk through the streets of Cherbourg. Note the colors, lighting, and composition as well as film techniques that give the sequence a romantic unreality.

In addition, there are films that attempt to reproduce the style of a particular painter or period, such as Stanley Kubrick's *Barry Lyndon* (Gainsborough, Watteau), Daniel Vigné's *The Return of Martin Guerre* (Brueghel), and Herbert Ross' *Pennies from Heaven*, which replicates some of Edward Hopper's most famous paintings.

Finally, we've identified a few films that depict painters or sculptors at work: the abstract expressionist painter in Martin Scorsese's section of *New York Stories*, van Gogh in *Vincent & Theo*, Michelangelo in *The Agony and the Ecstasy*, and the famous medieval Russian icon painter in *Andrei Rublev*.

Using Film in the Performing Arts

Music, dance, and drama have been an integral part of film since its earliest days. Here are some suggestions for incorporating film in these areas of the curriculum.

Dance. View dance sequences from such films as *Singin' in the Rain*, *Sarafina!*, *The Turning Point*, or any Busby Berkeley or Rogers and Astaire film. In addition to responding to the movements of the dancers, analyze the role of the cinematography and editing in presenting the dance, using the following questions:

1. Is the dance presented from a fixed place in the auditorium or are there cuts back and forth between long, medium, and close shots?

2. Are the shots from eye level or is there a combination of high- and low-angle shots as well?

3. Is the rhythmic pulse of the dance maintained by the choreography, by the editing, or by a combination of both?

4. To what extent do the cinematic elements work with or against the choreography?

5. Are the dances created directly for the screen (*Singin' in the Rain*, *Sarafina!*, *Fame*, *Footloose*, the films of Busby Berkeley and Astaire and Rogers) different from dances created for the stage and then filmed (*The Turning Point*)?

Music. Music is a vital element of most fiction films—from dramatic underscoring of nearly every scene to outright musicals.

In the first case—dramatic underscoring written expressly for a film sequence—examining film soundtrack music is a great opportunity for music students to explore the ability of music to evoke emotions. The following clips feature interesting uses of musical score. (Complete citations are in the filmography at the end of the chapter.)

- The second sequence in *The Road Warrior* [0:03:58 to 0:08:45] is a spectacular chase sequence with a driving, brassy score.
- Bernard Herrmann's "Waltz Theme and Variations" underscores the breakfast scene in *Citizen Kane* [0:50:45 to 0:53:55]. Incidentally, this music was composed prior to shooting the scene so that the dialogue and photography would cut in rhythm with the variations.
- Herrmann's music powerfully underscores Kim Novak's transformation scene in *Vertigo* [1:54:40 to 1:56:55].
- John Williams' ominous score for the credits and opening scene of *Jaws* [0:00:00 to 0:05:00]—may be clichéd, but it's still chilling.
- In John Williams' score for the first scene of *E. T.: The Extra-Terrestrial* [0:01:35 to 0:07:25], notice the difference between the music in the first part of the scene and the music after the arrival of the men.

Another category of film music includes classical music appropriated for dramatic underscoring, for example:

- Johann Pachelbel's Canon in D (*Ordinary People*)
- Tomaso Albinoni's Adagio (*Gallipoli*)
- Mozart's Piano Concerto No. 21 (*Elvira Madigan*)
- Johann Strauss' "Blue Danube Waltz" and Richard Strauss' *Also Sprach Zarathustra* (*2001: A Space Odyssey*)

Several activities with film clips allow students to draw conclusions about the use of music in film. These tend to work best with nondialogue scenes.

1. First, play only the audio for the sequence (turn the television's brightness control all the way down). Ask students what type of action they imagined from the combination of music and sound effects. What mood does the music set? What type of photography and editing would you expect in the scene? Then play the sequence again with the video. How does the actual scene match the students' predictions? In their opinion, is the music appropriate for

the scene? If the music is of the preexisting, classical variety, does the music match the historical setting of the film, as it does in such films as *Dangerous Liaisons* (Handel) or *Amadeus* (Mozart), or is it a deliberate mismatch, as it is in *A Clockwork Orange* (Rossini and Beethoven) and *2001: A Space Odyssey* (Johann Strauss and Richard Strauss).

2. Play a sequence of a film without any sound. What kind of music do students expect to accompany the scene: Fast or slow? Harmonious or discordant? Major or minor key? Classical or contemporary? Strings, brass, percussion, or whole orchestra?

3. Substitute a different type of music for the soundtrack music in a nonverbal sequence. For example, play a recording of a Mozart symphony during the opening chase of *The Road Warrior*. How does the new music affect the viewer's perception of the scene?

4. In all of these activities, explore the question: How does film music provide emotional cues?

In the second major category of film music, explore students' responses to musical numbers from film musicals. There are several categories to sample here: original film musicals of the 1930s through 1950s (*Footlight Parade, 42nd Street, Singin' in the Rain*, to name a few); adaptations of classic stage musicals (*Carousel, Gypsy, A Chorus Line*); and interesting contemporary variations like *Cabaret* (where the musical numbers are all set in a nightclub and comment on the action in the dramatic scenes), *Yentl* (in which the musical numbers serve as interior monologues for the main character), and *Pennies from Heaven* (where actors lip synch to old recordings of popular songs from the 1930s). Finally, there are films where music is a direct and vital concern of adolescents—either as a career (as in *Fame*) or as an outlet for self-expression (as in *Sing!* and *Shout*).

Using Films in Foreign Language Classrooms

Foreign language films are useful in second language classrooms both because they show the target language being spoken in context by native speakers and because they provide richly detailed historical or cultural background information. We recommend that foreign language teachers use both clips and whole films with viewing guides such as those described in Chapter Three. They may choose to add a section for "Unfamiliar Vocabulary" or "Aspects of Culture" or any other concept they are emphasizing. Whereas almost any film in a second language will suffice for these purposes, we've found that foreign language teachers are constantly looking for good stories about adolescent or young adult protagonists. The following lists are by no means complete, but provide a starting point for language teachers. (The films marked with an asterisk have young adult protagonists.)

French
*Au Revoir les Enfants**

Black Orpheus (Orfeu Negro)

*Cross My Heart (La Fracture du Myocarde)**

Danton

*The 400 Blows (Les Quatre Cents Coups)**

Jean de Florette/Manon of the Spring (Manon des Sources)

The King of Hearts (Le Roi de Coeur)

*La Boum**

*Life is a Long Quiet River (La Vie est une Longue Fleuve Tranquille)**

*My Father's Glory (La Gloire de Mon Pere)**

*My Mother's Castle (Le Chateau de Ma Mere)**

The Return of Martin Guerre (Le Retour de Martin Guerre)

*Sugar Cane Alley (Rue Cases Negres)**

*The Umbrellas of Cherbourg (Les Parapluies de Cherbourg)**

German
The Boat (Das Boot)

*Europa, Europa**

*The Nasty Girl (Das Schreckliche Mädchen)**

Italian
*The Bicycle Thief**

*Cinema Paradiso**

*The Night of the Shooting Stars**

Japanese
Ran

*The Samurai Trilogy**

Sanjuro

The Seven Samurai

Throne of Blood

Yojimbo

Russian

Alexander Nevksy

Andrei Rublev

Ivan the Terrible, Parts I and II

Spanish

*El Norte**

The Official Story

The Place of Film Study in the English/Language Arts Curriculum

In one sense, all of the other chapters of this book are about including film in the English curriculum, especially in terms of integrating viewing with reading, writing, speaking, and listening (Chapters One through Four) and including film in thematic units (Chapters Six through Ten). Here we consider three particular issues not covered elsewhere: (1) the "big picture"—the scope and sequence of film study in the secondary English curriculum, (2) general strategies for film/literature connections, and (3) the design of elective courses in mass communications or film study.

Scope and sequence. Based on our experience with teaching film in grades 6–12, we recommend the following sequence of film topics and activities in the secondary English/language arts curriculum. We have assumed that most states and districts require at least one course in American literature and one course in British literature. Since many states and districts (including ours) now require a course in "non-English" world literature, we have included such a course at grade 10. Needless to say, the order of the topics in grades 10 through 12 is flexible.

Grades	Focus/Topics/Activities
Grades 6–8	basic film terms applied to clips; viewer response of whole film as part of a thematic unit; writing film reviews (summary, evaluation, basic analysis)
Grade 9	more depth on film terminology; viewer response to whole film; analytical film reviews (including analysis of cinematic elements); introduction to film genres, perhaps focusing on one genre with a comparison essay (Detective genre is a good choice here if western and gangster films are included in the American literature course.)

Grade 10   "close viewing"—particularly of international films connected to world literature curriculum

Grade 11   thematic connections with works of American literature; American film genres in more depth, particularly western and gangster, possibly screwball comedy; classics of the silent era; *Citizen Kane* or another "nongenre" American film classic; documentaries about literary periods or specific authors

Grade 12   thematic connections with works of British literature; close viewing of more sophisticated films—particularly from Great Britain or the former British colonies; Shakespeare on film; in-depth exploration of tragedy, satire, romanticism, realism, and other such topics

Connecting film and literature. By now, readers have probably concluded that we have a rather strong bias against English teachers' routine showing of the entire film of a novel that the whole class has studied in depth, especially if the teacher's reason for showing the film is either (1) to prove the book was better (just tell the students and let them rent it at their own peril—why would you want to spend any class time with inferior material?); (2) to fill time between the unit test and the weekend (there *has* to be something more worthwhile for students to do); (3) to appease students who whine, beg, and plead (beware this jabberwock, my friend!); or (4) to engage in comparison and contrast writing or discussion. This last reason may surprise some readers, but we've found that such comparisons usually boil down to simplistic variations on a relatively few points: (1) "the filmmakers left stuff out" (yes, usually lots of characters and whole subplots have to go in order to whittle the novel down to two hours); (2) "they simplified complex material for the mass audience" (yes, literature is much better at conveying nuances and complexities—especially of characters' unexpressed thoughts and feelings); (3) "they toned down the controversial material" (as in the near absence of lesbianism in Spielberg's version of *The Color Purple*); or (4) "the actors weren't how we pictured the characters" (perhaps Demi Moore was not our first choice for Hester Prynne).

Actually, we believe that there are some interesting book and film pairs. For example, Harold Pinter's script for the film version of John Fowles' *The French Lieutenant's Woman* solves an interesting dilemma: How could a film version convey the narrator's voice and stance without resorting to clumsy voice-overs? The answer was to invent a whole new plot about contemporary actors who are making a film of a Victorian story. The actors' discussion of their characters and of the historical period provides commentary similar to that of the narrator in the novel. Still, for the most part, we recommend that teachers who want to teach a film alongside a novel consider one of the following types of pairings (always a high-quality film with a high-quality book).

- *A film set in the same country and period as the novel, but with a different focus.* For example, use *The Inner Circle* to supplement study of Alexander Solzhenitsyn's *One Day in the Life of Ivan Denisovich.* The film provides a view of Stalin's inner sanctum and the life of an ordinary person living "freely" in Moscow, which contrasts with life for Ivan in a Siberian prison camp. Similarly, while studying Hermann Hesse's *Siddhartha*, use the half of Bertolucci's *Little Buddha* that tells the story of the transformation of Prince Siddhartha into the Buddha.

- *A novel and a film adaptation of another novel by the same author.* A good pairing here is Roman Polanski's *Tess* with any other novel by Thomas Hardy. The excellent attention to costume and sets in *Tess* gives today's visually oriented adolescents images they can use while reading other novels set in Hardy's Wessex. American literature teachers who teach the short stories and shorter novels of John Steinbeck could use John Ford's beautiful adaptation of *The Grapes of Wrath* to provide images of the Great Depression in Oklahoma and California.

- *A novel and a film that share a similar situation or theme.* For example, the young men in Gabe Torres' *December* stay up all night deciding whether to enlist in the army following the 1941 attack on Pearl Harbor. Teachers could use all or part of this movie to supplement the study of John Knowles' *A Separate Peace.*

- *Books and films from the same literary genres, such as epic, tragedy, fairy tale, satire, or myths and legends.* Consider *Citizen Kane* as a tragedy and compare it with *Macbeth* or *Death of a Salesman.* Include Kubrick's *Dr. Strangelove* in a satire unit with *Gulliver's Travels.* *Black Orpheus* provides a modern adaptation of the myth of Orpheus and Eurydice set in Rio de Janeiro during Carnival.

- *Novels or plays and their "displaced" film adaptations.* In these pairs, the filmmakers have preserved the general plot, situation, characters, or theme of a literary work but have radically transposed other details, particularly the setting. Some examples are Conrad's *Heart of Darkness* and Coppola's *Apocalypse Now,* Austen's *Emma* and Heckerling's *Clueless, Romeo and Juliet* and Coolidge's *Valley Girl, King Lear* and Kurosawa's *Ran,* and *Cyrano de Bergerac* and Schepisi's *Roxanne.*

In what may seem a reversal of our strong bias against the knee-jerk practice of read-the-book-show-the-video, we assert that using good film or video versions of plays is preferable to merely reading the play. In our view, plays are meant to be seen and heard (preferably with a live audience), not read silently. The experience of having the play acted out, hearing the language of the author, and seeing authentic sets and costumes provides the next best thing to seeing a performance of the play. There are some excellent versions available of such frequently taught plays as *Cyrano de Bergerac, Death of a Salesman, A Raisin in the Sun,* and *The Miracle Worker,* to say nothing of the numerous adaptations of Shakespearean plays.

Effective strategies for presenting a film or video version of a play include:

1. Have students view an act or scene from the play with their written versions in front of them. Turn off the video and discuss the portion that you have seen, with students using their printed versions to refer to specific lines of dialogue.

2. Have students read a scene as homework prior to viewing the scene on video. Before showing the video, check to see what the students have understood about the scene and ask them to predict how the director of the film might have staged a particular bit of action. Find out what parts of the scene are unclear to the students. Then, view all or part of what they have read and discuss how the film version met their expectations, cleared up their confusion, or added a surprising interpretation.

3. Use the video as the students' first encounter with the play and have them reread the act or scene for homework, perhaps writing answers to specific questions. Routinely include this question: Did the filmmakers make any significant changes in the play?

4. Have the students read the whole play and show only key scenes from the video.

5. If the play has more than one video version available (as with the Shakespearean plays), have the students read the entire play, but show clips of key scenes from two different versions. For example, compare and contrast Hamlet's "To be or not to be" soliloquy as presented in the film versions with Sir Laurence Olivier (1948), Nicol Williamson (1969), and Mel Gibson (1990).

6. To go beyond having the film or video version of the play be merely a strategy for "inputting" the play, have students use a viewing guide (see Chapter Three). Routinely discuss how the director uses close-ups, camera angles, lighting, editing, and background music to add meaning to the dialogue.

Elective courses in film. Some secondary English departments offer elective courses in film, television, and other mass media. For a course in the art and history of film—either as a stand-alone course or as a unit of a mass communications course—we offer this list of topics from the first century of film history.

- the invention of film and its international beginnings
- the silent era (roughly 1895 to 1929)
- early sound films (1930s)
- classic Hollywood style (developed from 1930s to 1950s)
- film genres (westerns, detective films, etc.)
- movies as art, industry, business, and entertainment
- the movies' response to other media (television in the 1950s; video in the 1980s; and computers, laser disks, and CD-ROM technology in the 1990s)
- developments in postwar international cinema such as Italian neo-realism, the French "New Wave," Germany's "Third Generation," and the postwar emergence of Japanese and Chinese cinema
- case studies of directors (*auteur* criticism or *"politique des auteurs"*) using the films of directors such as Altman, Truffaut, Bergman, Fellini, and Hitchcock
- documentaries and avant garde films
- documentary films about the production of specific films ("The Making of . . ." films that are readily available on cable television and in video stores)
- feature films about filmmaking, such as *The Stunt Man, Last Action Hero, The Projectionist,* and *The Purple Rose of Cairo*

The issue of texts for secondary-school film courses is problematic. All of the better textbooks are aimed at the college audience. We believe that advanced high school students could successfully use Giannetti's *Understanding Movies* (1990) or Ron Johnson and Jan Bone's *Understanding the Film: An Introduction to Film Appreciation.* David Bordwell and Kristin Thompson's *Film Art: An Introduction* would definitely stretch most high school students. To our knowledge there are no general textbooks about film for middle school students.

Good supplementary materials for teachers include David A. Cook's *A History of Narrative Film,* Morris Beja's *Film & Literature: An Introduction,* Louis Giannetti's *Masters of the American Cinema* (1981), James Monaco's *How to Read a Film,* and Erik Barnouw's *Documentary: A History of the Non-Fiction Film.* Reference materials on film genres are cited at the end of Chapter Four.

Teachers of film electives will also want several instructional films to use with students: the PBS *American Cinema* series is extensive and excellent (and available in most video stores). Pyramid Films offers *Basic Film Terms: A Visual Dictionary, Basic Film Editing,* and *Basic Film Photography. Visions of Light* is a wonderful documentary on the work of several major cinematographers.

Notes

1. We acknowledge that it is important to teach students how to compose visually—from making charts and diagrams to display data and illustrate reports, to producing their own films and videos—and that we have chosen not to focus on visual composing in this book. We have taught students how to use a storyboard—both as a way of planning a film or video and as a general tool, much like flowcharts, for organizing information that combines text and visuals. With the increasing use of CD-ROM technology and the availability of reasonably priced camcorders and video editors, the means of producing student films and videos are available in many secondary schools. Although we offer a few suggestions for student-made visuals, a comprehensive treatment of visual composition is a topic for another book.

Bibliography for Chapter Five

Barchers, S. I. 1994. *Language Arts: An Integrated Approach.* St. Paul, MN: West Publishing Company.

Barnouw, E. 1983. *Documentary: A History of the Non-Fiction Film.* Oxford: Oxford University Press.

Bawden, L.-A., ed. 1976. *The Oxford Companion to Film.* New York: Oxford University Press.

Beja, M. 1979. *Film & Literature: An Introduction.* New York: Longman.

Bordwell, D., and K. Thompson. 1993. *Film Art: An Introduction.* 4th ed. New York: McGraw-Hill.

Carnes, M. C. 1995. "Hollywood History." *American Heritage* 46(September): 74–84.

Carnes, M. C., ed. 1995. *Past Imperfect: History According to the Movies.* New York: Henry Holt and Company.

Considine, D., and G. Haley. 1992. *Visual Messages: Integrating Imagery into Instruction.* Englewood, CO: Teachers Ideas Press.

Cook, D. A. 1981. *A History of Narrative Film.* New York: W. W. Norton & Company.

Costanzo, W. V., ed. 1987. Report by NCTE Committee on Film Study in American Schools. ERIC Document No. ED 287 165.

Costanzo, W. V. 1992. *Reading the Movies: Twelve Great Films on Video and How to Teach Them.* Urbana, IL: National Council of Teachers of English.

Cox, C. 1985. "Filmmaking as a Composing Process." *Language Arts*, 62(June): 60–69.

Foster, H. M. 1979. *The New Literacy*. Urbana, IL: National Council of Teachers of English.

Franek, M. 1996. "Producing Student Films: Shakespeare on Screen." *English Journal*, 85(March): 50–54.

Giannetti, L. 1981. *Masters of the American Cinema*. Englewood Cliffs, NJ: Prentice-Hall, Inc.

Giannetti, L. 1987. *Understanding Movies*. 4th ed. Englewood Cliffs, NJ: Prentice-Hall, Inc.

Giannetti, L. 1990. *Understanding Movies*. 5th ed. Englewood Cliffs, NJ: Prentice-Hall, Inc.

Greenspan, J. 1993. *Careers for Film Buffs and Other Hollywood Types*. Lincolnwood, IL: NTC Publishing Group.

Jawitz, W. 1996. *Understanding Mass Media*. 5th ed. Lincolnwood, IL: National Textbook Company.

Johnson, R., and J. Bone. 1986. *Understanding the Film: An Introduction to Film Appreciation*. 3rd ed. Lincolnwood, IL: National Textbook Company.

Mejia, E., M. K. Xiao, and J. Kennedy. 1994. *102 Very Teachable Films*. Englewood Cliffs, NJ: Prentice-Hall Regents.

Monaco, J. 1981. *How to Read a Film*. New York: Oxford University Press.

North Carolina. 1992. *Competency-Based Curriculum Teacher Handbook, English Language Arts K–12*. Raleigh, NC: Department of Public Instruction.

Sinatra, R. 1986. *Visual Connections to Thinking, Reading, and Writing*. Springfield, IL: Charles C. Thomas.

Suhor, C. 1991. "Report on Trends and Issues." Urbana, IL: National Council of Teachers of English.

Wheeler, D., ed. 1989. *No, But I Saw the Movie: The Best Short Stories Ever Made into Film*. New York: Penguin Books.

Films Cited in Chapter Five

Information provided for each film is title, country (if other than the United States), director, year of release, MPAA rating, length, and language (if other than English). Films are arranged alphabetically by title within each group.

Social Studies

Alexander Nevsky, Russia, Sergei Eisenstein, 1938, NR, 107 min., in Russian.

The Battleship Potemkin, Russia, Sergei Eisenstein, 1925, NR, 71 min., silent with English titles.

The Black Robe, Canada, Bruce Beresford, 1991, R, 101 min.

Cry Freedom, Richard Attenborough, 1987, PG, 157 min.

"The Civil War," Ken Burns, 1990, nine episodes, total 680 min.

Danton, France, Andrzej Wajda, 1982, PG, 136 min., in French.

Das Boot (The Boat), Germany, Wolfgang Petersen, 1981, R, 145 min., in German.

A Dry White Season, South Africa, Euzhan Palcy, 1989, R, 115 min., in English (some Afrikaans and Bantu).

El Norte, Gregory Nava, 1983, R, 139 min., in English and Spanish.

Europa, Europa, Germany, Agnieszka Holland, 1991, R, 115 min., in German.

"Eyes on the Prize," Blackside, Inc. Productions, Judith Vecchione, Senior Producer, 1987, 7 volumes, NR, approximately 14 hrs.

Gallipoli, Australian, Peter Weir, 1981, PG, 111 min.

Gandhi, Richard Attenborough, 1982, PG, 188 min.

Glory, Edward Zwick, 1989, R, 122 min.

Henry V, Kenneth Branagh, 1989, NR, 138 min.

The Inner Circle, Andrei Konchalovsky, 1991, PG-13, 122 min.

Ivan the Terrible, Parts I and II, Russia, Sergei Eisenstein, 1946, NR, 186 min., in Russian.

The King of Hearts, France, Philippe De Broca, 1966, NR, 102 min., in French and English.

Korczak, Poland, Andrzej Wajda, 1990, NR, 113 min., in Polish.

The Last Emperor, Bernardo Bertolucci, 1987, PG-13, 164 min.

Legends of the Fall, Edward Zwick, 1994, R, 124 min.

The Long Walk Home, George Fenton, 1989, PG, 95 min.

Malcolm X, Spike Lee, 1992, PG-13, 201 min.

Missing, Constantin Costa-Gavras, 1982, PG, 122 min.

The Nasty Girl (Das Schreckliche Mädchen), Germany, Michael Verhoeven, 1990, PG-13, 94 min., in German.

The Night of the Shooting Stars, Italy, Paolo and Vittorio Taviani, 1982, PG, 106 min., in Italian.

The Official Story, Argentina, Luis Puenzo, 1985, PG, 110 min., in Spanish.

A Passage to India, David Lean, 1984, PG, 163 min.

Peter the Great, Marvin Chomsky and Lawrence Schiller, 1986, NR, 371 min.

The Power of One, John G. Avildsen, 1992, PG-13, 127 min.

The Return of Martin Guerre, France, Daniel Vigne, 1982, NR, 111 min., in French.

Roots, David Greene and others, 1977, NR, 570 min., six episodes.

Samurai Trilogy, Japan, Hiroshi Inagaki, NR, in Japanese. Individual films are *Musashi Miyamoto* (1954, 92 min.), *Duel at Ichijoji Temple* (1955, 102 min.), and *Duel at Ganryu Island* (1956, 102 min.).

Sanjuro, Japan, Akira Kurosawa, 1962, NR, 96 min., in Japanese.

Sarafina!, South Africa, Darrell James Roodt, 1992, PG-13, 98 min.

Schindler's List, Steven Spielberg, 1993, R, 195 min., in English, German, and Polish.

The Seven Samurai, Japan, Akira Kurosawa, 1954, NR, 204 min., in Japanese.

A World Apart, Chris Menges, 1988, PG, 135 min.

Yojimbo, Japan, Akira Kurosawa, 1961, NR, 110 min., in Japanese.

Science

Apollo 13, Ron Howard, 1995, PG, 140 min.

Lorenzo's Oil, George Miller, 1992, PG-13, 136 min.

Never Cry Wolf, Carroll Ballard, 1983, PG, 105 min.

Math

Stand and Deliver, Ramon Menendez, 1988, PG, 105 min.

Visual Arts

The Agony and the Ecstasy, Carol Reed, 1965, NR, 136 min.

Akira Kurosawa's Dreams, Akira Kurosawa, 1990, PG, 120 min., in Japanese.

Andrei Rublev, Andrei Tarkovsky, 1966, NR, 185 min., in Russian.

Barry Lyndon, Stanley Kubrick, 1975, PG, 185 min.

New York Stories, Martin Scorsese, Francis Ford Coppola, and Woody Allen, 1989, PG, 124 min.

Pennies from Heaven, Herbert Ross, 1981, R, 107 min.

The Return of Martin Guerre, France, Daniel Vigné, 1982, NR, 111 min., in French.

The Umbrellas of Cherbourg (Les Parapluies de Cherbourg), France, Jacques Demy, 1964, NR, 90 min., in French.

Vincent & Theo, Robert Altman, 1990, PG-13, 138 min.

Performing Arts: Dance

Fame, Alan Parker, 1980, R, 133 min.

Footloose, Herbert Ross, 1984, PG, 107 min.

Sarafina!, South Africa, Darrell James Roodt, 1992, PG-13, 98 min.

Singin' in the Rain, Gene Kelly and Stanley Donen, 1952, NR, 103 min.

The Turning Point, Herbert Ross, 1977, PG, 119 min.

Performing Arts: Music

Amadeus, Milos Forman, 1984, PG, 158 min.

Cabaret, Bob Fosse, 1972, PG, 119 min.

Carousel, Henry King, 1956, NR, 128 min.

A Chorus Line, Richard Attenborough, 1985, PG-13, 118 min.

Citizen Kane, Orson Welles, 1941, NR, 119 min.

A Clockwork Orange, Stanley Kubrick, 1971, R, 137 min.

Dangerous Liaisons, Stephen Frears, 1988, R, 120 min.

Elvira Madigan, Sweden, Bo Widerberg, 1967, PG, 89 min., in Swedish.

E.T.: The Extra-Terrestrial, Steven Spielberg, 1982, PG, 115 min.

Fame, Alan Parker, 1980, R, 133 min.

Footlight Parade, Lloyd Bacon, 1933, NR, 104 min.

42nd Street, Lloyd Bacon, 1933, NR, 89 min.

Gallipoli, Australian, Peter Weir, 1981, PG, 111 min.

Gypsy, Mervyn LeRoy, 1962, NR, 144 min.

Jaws, Steven Spielberg, 1975, PG, 124 min.

Ordinary People, Robert Redford, 1980, R, 123 min.

Pennies from Heaven, Herbert Ross, 1981, R, 107 min.

The Road Warrior, George Miller, 1982, R, 95 min.

Shout, Jeffrey Hornaday, 1991, PG-13, 93 min.

Sing!, Richard Baskin, 1989, PG-13, 111 min.

Singin' in the Rain, Gene Kelly and Stanley Donen, 1952, NR, 103 min.

2001: A Space Odyssey, Stanley Kubrick, 1968, NR, 139 min.

Vertigo, Alfred Hitchcock, 1958, PG, 126 min.

Yentl, Barbra Streisand, 1983, PG, 134 min.

Foreign Languages

French

Au Revoir les Enfants, France, Louis Malle, 1987, PG, 104 min.

Black Orpheus, France (filmed in Brazil), Marcel Camus, 1958, NR, 103 min., in Portuguese and French.

Cross My Heart (La Fracture du Myocarde), France, Jacques Fansten, 1992, NR, 105 min.

Danton, France, Andrzej Wajda, 1982, PG, 136 min.

The 400 Blows, France, François Truffaut, 1959, NR, 99 min.

Jean de Florette/Manon of the Spring, France, Claude Berri, 1987, PG/PG-13, 122min./113 min.

The King of Hearts, France, Philippe De Broca, 1966, NR, 102 min., in French and English.

La Boum, France, Claude Pinoteau, 1980, NR, 100 min.

Life Is a Long Quiet River, France, Etienne Chatiliez, 1987, NR, 89 min.

My Father's Glory/My Mother's Castle, France, Yves Robert, 1991, G/PG, 110 min./98 min.

The Return of Martin Guerre, France, Daniel Vigné, 1982, NR, 111 min.

Sugar Cane Alley (Rue Cases Negres), Martinique, Euzhan Palcy, 1983, NR, 100 min.

Umbrellas of Cherbourg (Les Parapluies de Cherbourg), France, Jacques Demy, 1964, NR, 90 min.

German

Das Boot (The Boat), Germany, Wolfgang Petersen, 1981, R, 145 min.

Europa, Europa, Germany, Agnieszka Holland, 1991, R, 115 min.

The Nasty Girl (Das Schreckliche Mädchen), Germany, Michael Verhoeven, 1990, PG-13, 94 min.

Italian

The Bicycle Thief, Italy, Vittorio De Sica, 1949, NR, 90 min.

Cinema Paradiso, Italy, Giuseppe Tornatore, 1989, NR, 123 min.

The Night of the Shooting Stars, Italy, Paolo and Vittorio Taviani, 1982, PG, 106 min.

Japanese

Ran, Japan, Akira Kurosawa, 1985, R, 160 min.

Samurai Trilogy, Japan, Hiroshi Inagaki, NR. Individual films are *Musashi Miyamoto* (1954, 92 min.), *Duel at Ichijoji Temple* (1955, 102 min.), and *Duel at Ganryu Island* (1956, 102 min.).

Sanjuro, Japan, Akira Kurosawa, 1962, NR, 96 min.

The Seven Samurai, Japan, Akira Kurosawa, 1954, NR, 204 min.

Throne of Blood, Japan, Akira Kurosawa, 1957, NR, 105 min.

Yojimbo, Japan, Akira Kurosawa, 1961, NR, 110 min.

Russian

Alexander Nevsky, Russia, Sergei Eisenstein, 1938, NR, 107 min.

Andrei Rublev, Andrei Tarkovsky, 1966, NR, 185 min.

Ivan the Terrible, Parts I and II, Russia, Sergei Eisenstein, 1946, NR, 186 min.

Spanish

El Norte, Gregory Nava, 1983, R, 139 min., in English and Spanish.

The Official Story, Argentina, Luis Puenzo, 1985, PG, 110 min.

English/Language Arts

Apocalypse Now, Francis Ford Coppola, 1979, R, 153 min.

Black Orpheus, France (filmed in Brazil), Marcel Camus, 1958, NR, 103 min., in Portuguese and French.

Citizen Kane, Orson Welles, 1941, NR, 119 min.

Clueless, Amy Heckerling, 1995, PG-13, 97 min.

The Color Purple, Steven Spielberg, 1985, PG-13, 154 min.

Cyrano de Bergerac, Carl Foreman, 1950, NR, 112 min.

Cyrano de Bergerac, France, Jean-Paul Rappeneau, 1990, PG, 135 min., in French.

Death of a Salesman, Volker Schlondorff, 1986, NR, 135 min.

December, Gabe Torres, 1991, PG, 92 min.

Dr. Strangelove, or: How I Learned to Stop Worrying and Love the Bomb, Stanley Kubrick, 1964, NR, 93 min.

The French Lieutenant's Woman, Karel Reisz, 1981, R, 124 min.

The Grapes of Wrath, John Ford, 1940, NR, 129 min.

Hamlet, Laurence Olivier, 1948, NR, 153 min.

Hamlet, Tony Richardson, 1969, G, 114 min.

Hamlet, Franco Zeffirelli, 1990, PG, 135 min.

The Inner Circle, US (filmed in Russia), Andrei Konchalovsky, 1991, PG-13, 122 min.

Last Action Hero, John McTiernan, 1993, PG-13, 131 min.

Little Buddha, Bernardo Bertolucci, 1993, PG, 123 min.

The Miracle Worker, Arthur Penn, 1972, NR, 107 min.

The Projectionist, Harry Hurwitz, 1971, PG, 84 min.

The Purple Rose of Cairo, Woody Allen, 185, PG, 82 min.

A Raisin in the Sun, Daniel Petrie, 1961, NR, 128 min.

A Raisin in the Sun, Bill Duke, 1989, NR, 171 min.

Ran, Japan, Akira Kurosawa, 1985, R, 160 min., in Japanese.

Roxanne, Fred Schepisi, 1987, PG, 103 min.

The Stunt Man, Richard Rush, 1980, R, 129 min.

Tess, Roman Polanski, 1980, PG, 170 min.

Valley Girl, Martha Coolidge, 1983, R, 95 min.

Films About Filmmaking

American Cinema (The Annenberg/CPB Collection, 1994). This was a ten-episode documentary shown on PBS in 1994 and is available on five videocassettes. There is an additional cassette, available only by mail from Annenberg, with three short segments ("Film Language," "Writing and Thinking About Film," and "Classical Hollywood Style Today"), the first two of which would be effective with secondary students. (The Annenberg/CPB Collection, PO Box 2345, S. Burlington, VT 05407-2345, telephone 800-532-7637).

Basic Film Editing, Paul Burnford and Jerry Samuelson, 1975, NR, 17 min. (Available from Pyramid Film and Video, Box 1048, Santa Monica, CA 90406-1048, telephone 800-421-2304.)

Basic Film Photography, Paul Burnford and Jerry Samuelson, 1976, NR, 17 min. (Also available from Pyramid Film and Video.)

Basic Film Terms: A Visual Dictionary, Sheldon Renan, 1970, NR, 14 min. (Also available from Pyramid Film and Video.)

Visions of Light: The Art of Cinematography, Todd McCarthy, Stuart Samuels, and Arnold Glassman, 1992, NR, 95 min.

Introduction to Part II

In the first part of this book, we propose a framework for teaching film, strategies for teaching a single film, as well as strategies for teaching groups of related films. In Chapter Five, we address ways of teaching film across the curriculum and connecting film with classic works of literature.

In Part II, we discuss specifically a body of films we call "young adult films," analogous to the young adult novels used in our English and language arts classes—films that students will enjoy and that are appropriate for students to analyze and evaluate. We suggest ways of incorporating these films into the English/language arts curriculum by describing thematic units that use young adult films and by presenting a number of films within each theme.

As we set out to find films that would work well with young adults in the classroom, we checked video guides and perused the shelves of video rental stores, and we found more than eighty films. In identifying these films, we noticed five recurring themes that appear frequently in films about young people:

- coming of age
- families and family relationships
- belonging
- dreams and quests
- love and romance

When we analyzed all the films in a particular thematic group, we found three to five essential attributes that appear in almost all the films of a given theme. We recommend that teachers use these attributes in analyzing and discussing the films.

Each of the following five chapters contains an annotated list of films, a discussion of the essential attributes common to the films of each theme, and suggested writing activities. Some films clearly have multiple themes and could be used in several places, so we have included the annotation in the chapter where the film first appears and listed the film without annotation in the later chapters. For teachers who wish to connect the study of film with YA literature, Appendix B contains a list of recommended YA novels for each of the themes in Chapters Six through Ten.

Selection Criteria for Films in Part II

In recommending films to use with young adults, we have employed the following criteria:

1. *The protagonist of the film is ten to nineteen years old.* Our primary focus is films that deal with adolescent protagonists. Occasionally we have included a film with a younger or older protagonist because it deals with issues that are still pertinent to adolescents and because of its proven effectiveness with students.

2. *The film deals with issues of concern to adolescents.* We have identified films that deal with questions of coming of age, family relationships, belonging, dreams and quests, and love and romance. Typically we have not considered horror, fantasy, or martial arts films.

3. *The film is "teachable," that is, artful enough to warrant class time or student study.* We have excluded films with overly formulaic plots, schmaltzy narrations, or gratuitous sex and violence. We have asked ourselves: Can you imagine using this film in class? If the answer is no, we haven't included it. (Note: We have not automatically excluded films because of their MPAA rating. See our discussion of this issue in Chapter One, "Principles for Selection of Films.")

4. *The film is not an adaptation of a "classic" or of a widely read YA novel.* Because we want to encourage teachers to move away from the practice of showing films of novels studied in class, in these chapters we have deliberately excluded film adaptations of the high school canon. Hence, the lists don't include *The Outsiders, A Separate Peace,* or either version of *Lord of the Flies.*

5. *As a group, the films present a wide variety of protagonists, settings, and issues.* Since there were initially more films with white, middle-class boys, we have looked particularly for films that would give the list gender, ethnic, geographic, and historical diversity.

Chapter Six

Coming of Age

In selecting films appropriate to the theme of coming of age, we noticed three essential attributes that we almost always find in these films:

1. There is growth through the loss of innocence and the acquisition of knowledge.

2. A parent or mentor plays a role in this growth.

3. There are rituals or rites of passage involved in moving to adulthood.

Annotated List of Films

Information provided for each film is title, country (if other than the United States), director, year of release, MPAA rating, length, and language (if other than English). Films are in alphabetical order by title.

Alan & Naomi (Sterling VanWagenen, 1991, PG, 95 min.)

Alan is a Jewish boy living in New York at the end of World War II. When Alan would rather be playing stickball in the streets, his parents make him spend time with Naomi, a French refugee whose experiences in Nazi-occupied France have left her catatonic. Alan and Naomi develop a friendship that helps her begin to live and trust again.

Big (Penny Marshall, 1988, PG, 98 min.)

At a carnival fortune-telling booth, a twelve-year-old boy wishes "to be big." The next morning he wakes up in the body of a twenty-something-year-old. He's both frightened and thrilled. He finds a job as a toy consultant in a big company, where his ability to evaluate toys from a kid's perspective is highly prized and his boyish innocence is irresistible. He gets his own apartment and a grown-up girlfriend, but he misses his mom, his young friends, and his adolescence.

Brighton Beach Memoirs (Gene Saks, 1987, PG-13, 110 min.)

"I'm putting all this down in my memoirs so that if I grow up twisted and warped, the world will know why," says Eugene Jerome at the beginning of this film adaptation of Neil Simon's autobiographical play, the first in a trilogy that includes *Biloxi Blues* and *Broadway Bound*. It's Brooklyn in 1937, and Eugene lives with his parents, brother, aunt, and cousins. He fantasizes alternately about being a baseball player and a writer. Meanwhile, the family deals with the Depression, unemployment, the impending war, and the fate of their Jewish relatives in Eastern Europe.

Cinema Paradiso (Italy, Giuseppe Tornatore, 1989, NR, 123 min., in Italian.)

Salvatore, growing up in Sicily in the years following World War II, is drawn to the local theater, Cinema Paradiso. The projectionist, Alfredo, befriends Salvatore, watches over him as he grows toward manhood, and encourages him to leave Sicily for a career in film. As an adult, Salvatore returns to his village after becoming a successful director. The last scene—a montage of kisses from decades of films— is a must for all lovers of film

Crooklyn (Spike Lee, 1994, PG-13, 112 min.)

Troy Carmichael is the only girl in a family of five children growing up in Brooklyn in the 1970s. Through a series of episodes, the film provides a nostalgic portrait of the life of this middle-class African American family as they cope with everything from complaining neighbors to the death of the children's mother. Strong family relationships, humor, and a lively sound track combine to make this a very teachable film.

Dark Horse (David Hemmings, 1992, PG, 95 min.)

Fifteen-year-old Allie has a difficult time coping with the death of her mother followed by the family's move from Los Angeles to a small town. She gets in with the wrong crowd in her new school and eventually lands in trouble with the law. As part of her probation she works weekends on a horse farm, where she meets Jet, a wild-spirited horse who has been resistant to training. Girl and horse tame each other in this film about overcoming loss and growing up.

The Emerald Forest (John Boorman, 1985, R, 110 min.)

An American businessman and his family live in Brazil while he works on a project that involves cutting down part of the rain forest for development. One day his young son disappears into the forest, kidnapped by a tribe of Indians known for their "invisibility." Ten years later, the father encounters his son, now completely assimilated by the Indians. For the son, the father is the living manifestation of "Dadeh," a dream from his childhood. This is an excellent film to use in a discussion of cultural differences or of the meaning of civilization. (The R rating is the result of the natural nudity of the native people and a few sexual situations.)

Empire of the Sun (Steven Spielberg, 1987, PG, 153 min.)

Jamie, an English boy, is separated from his parents in Shanghai, China, at the beginning of World War II. Jamie spends four years in an internment camp, where his time is divided between helping the other British prisoners cope with deprivation and learning survival tips from fellow prisoner and American con artist, Basie. With a strong young male protagonist, this is a great film to teach. It is visually stunning and the story lends itself to good class discussion.

The 400 Blows (France, François Truffaut, 1959, NR, 99 min., in French.)

Twelve-year-old Antoine Doinel is having a troubled adolescence: conflict with and between his parents, boring and irrelevant teachers, and brushes with the law for petty crimes. This enduring classic of the French New Wave provides an excellent contrast with more contemporary films about teenagers.

Gallipoli (Australia, Peter Weir, 1981, PG, 111 min.)

In 1915, two young Australian runners go from rivalry to friendship as they set off together to join the Australian army in its fight against the Turks at Gallipoli. One of the young men, Archie Hamilton, has defied his parents and lied about his age to join the prestigious Light Horse Cavalry. The film follows the two soldiers through basic training in Cairo to the trenches of Gallipoli, where the harsh reality of war replaces their dreams of glory.

Hope and Glory (Great Britain, John Boorman, 1987, PG-13, 118 min.)

Billy Rowan spends World War II in London during the Blitz, and through his eyes this film documents the lives of the members of Billy's family: his father, Clive, who dreams of fighting for England, but becomes an army clerk instead; his mother, Grace, who holds her family together during the bombing; and his sister, Dawn, who comes of age and marries a Canadian flyer. Another noteworthy character is Billy's grandfather, who is simultaneously irascible and lovable.

The Inkwell (Matty Rich, 1994, R, 112 min.)

Sixteen-year-old Drew Tate worries his parents. His only friend is a doll his grandfather made for him when Drew was a child, and his parents suspect him of trying to burn down their home. In the summer of 1976, when the Tate family visits relatives in the Inkwell, a black enclave on Martha's Vineyard, Drew's presence creates some tension among family members. On the island, Drew meets several older women who recognize his good qualities and give him the confidence to make friends and to relate to his parents. This film portrays a boy's coming of age as well as a strong sense of family; moreover, it demonstrates that families can work to solve their problems by talking and listening to each other.

King of the Hill (Steven Soderberg, 1993, PG-13, 102 min.)

Based on the memoirs of A. E. Hochner, this film is set in 1933 during the height of the Depression. Twelve-year-old Aaron Kurlander and his family live in a rundown residential hotel in St. Louis. Aaron is clearly a bright, imaginative young man who hides his poverty by lying about his address and inventing professions for his parents. When Aaron's father cannot find steady work and his mother is sent to a tuberculosis sanitarium, Aaron's younger brother goes to live with relatives. After his father leaves for out-of-town work, Aaron must survive on his own. The film provides a vivid glimpse of life during the Depression as seen through the eyes of a child, but it also portrays the sense of desperation felt by many Americans during this period of our history.

The Learning Tree (Gordon Parks, 1969, PG, 107 min.)

Newt Winger, a fifteen-year-old black boy, comes of age during the 1920s in Kansas. In the course of this episodic film, based on Parks's autobiographical novel, Newt falls in love for the first time, faces a bully, and struggles against the expectations of the school system. For example, a white teacher discourages him from taking a college prep course of study because, "Negroes generally don't go to college, and if they do, they usually end up as porters." (Note: The language contains racial epithets.)

My Brilliant Career (Australia, Gillian Armstrong, 1979, G, 102 min.)

Sybilla is a headstrong girl in late nineteenth-century Australia. She goes to live with her grandmother on a large ranch in the Outback and has difficulty conforming to the expectations of young ladies of the time. She falls in love with a dashing young man and eventually must choose between settling down with him and pursuing her own calling as writer and teacher.

The Outside Chance of Maximilian Glick (Canada, Allan A. Goldstein, 1988, G, 92 min.)

In the early 1960s, Max faces his fourteenth birthday (and bar mitzvah) as one of the few Jews in the remote Canadian town of Beausejour. Through a humorous yet believable series of experiences, Max learns important lessons about fitting in, being true to oneself, and becoming a man.

The Power of One (John G. Avildsen, 1992, PG-13, 127 min.)

Based on the novel by Bryce Courtney, this film tells the story of P. K., an English boy born in South Africa in 1930. Orphaned as a child, P. K. comes of age in a prison under the dual tutelage of an elderly German pianist and a black boxing trainer. Because of stories told by the trainer, P. K. becomes something of a myth to the blacks—the "rainmaker" who will unite the tribes and bring harmony. In 1948, as P. K. prepares to go to Oxford, he joins a movement to resist apartheid.

Rich in Love (Bruce Beresford, 1993, PG-13, 105 min.)

Lucille is a high school senior when, with no warning, her mother leaves the family. The other family members—Lucille's father and her older sister—are astounded and hurt by the loss of their wife and mother, but Lucille is profoundly affected by her mother's departure. It is through her eyes that we watch the dissolution of this family in spite of Lucille's attempts to take her mother's place. Set in Charleston, South Carolina, this film is an interesting study of a family trying to hold together in a crisis.

Roots (Episode 1, David Greene, 1977, NR, 99, min.)

The first episode of the television miniseries adaptation of Alex Haley's family epic is set in Gambia, West Africa, in the few years preceding Kunta Kinte's capture in 1767 by slave traders. This episode is notable for its depiction of family life in eighteenth-century Africa, including the manhood training rituals Kunta endures just prior to his capture.

Sarafina! (South Africa, Darrell James Roodt, 1992, PG-13, 98 min.)

This adaptation of the Broadway musical focuses on the struggle of black youth in South Africa under apartheid. In 1986, young Sarafina dreams of the day when Nelson Mandela will be freed from prison, but the students in her Soweto school are drawn inexorably into violence. Sarafina comes to an awareness of the risks of taking a stand, of the cost of not taking a stand, and of conflicts between the principles of liberation and nonviolent resistance. The film has disturbing scenes of torture and violence, but it is one of the few films to tell this story from the point of view of a black teenager.

Sitting in Limbo (Canada, John N. Smith, 1986, PG, 95 min.)

This film documents the relationship of high school students Pat and Fabian, a black couple living in Montreal. Pat faces impending motherhood while Fabian drops out of high school to find work. In the months the film covers, Pat and Fabian learn a great deal about the reality of life as they cope with a shady landlord, a tight budget, and adult responsibilities. The characters and situations in this film are compelling.

This Is My Life (Nora Ephron, 1992, PG, 94 min.)

Single mom Dottie Ingels is a saleswoman at Bloomingdales who dreams of being a stand-up comedian. As her comedy career takes off, her daughters have to grow up without her. It's especially hard on Erica, the fifteen-year-old; ten-year-old Opal seems a bit more resilient. Funny and sentimental, the film is full of wry observations on growing up and on parent/child relationships.

28 Up (Great Britain, Michael Apted, 1985, NR, 136 min.)

This documentary chronicles the lives of a group of English twenty-eight-year-olds who were first interviewed at age seven. Clips from interviews with the young people at ages seven, fourteen, twenty-one, and now at age twenty-eight show good insight into the levels of English society and the paths these different individuals' lives have taken.

The Essential Attributes of Coming-of-Age Films

Growth Through Loss of Innocence and Acquisition of Knowledge

In coming-of-age films, the protagonist grows in some way. This growth may manifest itself in the protagonist's beginning the film as a child and ending it as an adult, but more often the growth involves gaining understanding—a mature understanding that he or she must have to be an adult. With the understanding often comes a loss of innocence. When P. K., in *The Power of One*, gains knowledge of the injustice of apartheid, he loses his innocence. When Jamie (*Empire of the Sun*) spends four years in a Japanese internment camp, he leaves his childhood behind while learning the adult skills necessary to keep him alive. In *Crooklyn*, the death of her mother takes away Troy Carmichael's childhood and places *her* in the role of mother for her four brothers. Canadian teenagers Pat and Fabian (*Sitting in Limbo*) actually enter the adult world and take on the responsibilities of parenthood. In so doing, they gain new knowledge about the world. By dealing with an unscrupulous landlord and having to live on a budget that allows no nonessentials, Pat and Fabian learn that life can be hard and unfair. The knowledge brings about a loss of innocence for these two young people.

The protagonist's growth can be the result of a first experience with love or a first sexual encounter. For example, in a humorous but painfully realistic scene, Erica (*This Is My Life*) falls in love and fumbles through her first sexual encounter. In *The Inkwell*, an older woman helps Drew Tate grow up, first by listening to and respecting him and then, we are led to believe, by teaching him about lovemaking.

Occasionally the protagonist in coming-of-age films takes on adult roles because of the demands of circumstance, and when the circumstances are removed, resumes the role of a child. Jamie, in *Empire of the Sun*, provides for and protects the older British prisoners in the Japanese internment camp. When the Americans begin the bombing that ultimately brings about the end of World War II— and of his life in the camp—Jamie becomes a child again and cries for the first time in years. A more vivid example occurs in the fantasy *Big* when a thirteen-year-old actually attains adult size overnight. He becomes a business executive and even has a sexual encounter, but when his normal size is restored, he is delighted to be a child again.

The Role of a Parent, Mentor, or Guide

Protagonists in coming-of-age films often have adults—parents, mentors, or guides—who accompany the youth or serve as a source of wisdom. Salvatore, the young hero of *Cinema Paradiso*, learns to love films from Alfredo, the projectionist at the local movie theater. The older man actually makes it possible for Salvatore to leave his small Italian town and eventually move to Rome to become a filmmaker. In *The Outside Chance of Maximilian Glick*, a rabbi serves as a mentor for young Max, helping interpret the actions and attitudes of the adults around him. For Archie Hamilton in *Gallipoli*, the guide is his uncle, whose words of advice ring in his ears even as Archie runs to his death at the battle of Gallipoli.

Rituals or Rites of Passage

Protagonists in coming-of-age films often participate in some ritual of adulthood or rite of passage. We have found that talking with students about rites of passage is often difficult, because our contemporary American society has so few clearly defined rituals for becoming an adult. In fact, we can only think of one universal rite of adulthood for American teenagers: obtaining a driver's license. For some teenagers, graduating from high school or opening a checking account in a bank may also qualify as rites of passage. Defining rituals for our students and providing them with examples from other cultures help students locate rituals in their own experience. One example of a rite of passage is in the first episode of *Roots*, in which Kunta Kinte, along with other teenage boys from his village, is taken to an isolated area where he is taught what it means to be a man. When these young men return to their village, they take their place as men. For example, Kunta no longer defers to his mother, but he gives her orders as befits a man in his village.

Rituals of adulthood are often subtle in YA films. Sybilla (*My Brilliant Career*) spends time with her grandmother on the older woman's ranch in Australia, learning the expectations for young women of the nineteenth century. A bar mitzvah serves as a rite of passage for young Max in *The Outside of Chance of Maximilian Glick*. Billy Rowan (*Hope and Glory*) participates in rituals of adulthood both personally and vicariously as he experiences life during the London Blitz and as he observes his sister, Dawn, pass into adulthood.

Writing Assignments

1. Watch *28 Up*, a documentary that consists of interviews with a group of English young people at the age of twenty-eight and also shows clips of them at ages seven, fourteen, and twenty-one. Then, write an essay analyzing the issues confronted by these young people as they come of age.

2. Select two coming-of-age films that are, on the surface, quite different. Write a paper comparing and contrasting the films using the essential attributes as points of comparison.

3. Take the essential attributes for films dealing with coming of age and apply them to one film from the list. Then, explain how the film conforms to or deviates from the attributes.

4. Compare the wartime experiences of Archie Hamilton *(Gallipoli)* and Richie Perry in Walter Dean Myers' novel *Fallen Angels*.

5. Compare and contrast the treatment of boys' and girls' coming of age as portrayed in film or literature. Films to consider include *My Brilliant Career, Crooklyn,* and *This Is My Life* for girls; and *The Outside Chance of Maximilian Glick, Brighton Beach Memoirs,* and *The Emerald Forest* for boys.

6. Identify a person who has been instrumental to you in growing up. Write a letter to that person thanking him or her and identifying specifically what you have learned.

7. Compare and contrast the "good" mentors in *The Power of One* with Justin McLeod in Isabelle Holland's *The Man without a Face* or with Dakota in *Running Loose* by Chris Crutcher.

8. Compare and contrast two harmful mentors—for example, Basie in *Empire of the Sun* and Gary Lawlor in Terry Davis' *If Rock and Roll Were a Machine*.

9. Consider the rites of passage in Episode 1 of *Roots* and in Gary Paulsen's *Hatchet*. Then, explain what it means to be a man, rather than a boy, in each of these works.

10. Sometimes circumstances force characters to take on the role of an adult, and when the circumstances are removed, the characters revert to their childlike behaviors. Compare and contrast the effect of this "forced adulthood" on Jamie in *Empire of the Sun* or Josh in *Big* with the boys in William Golding's novel *Lord of the Flies*.

Chapter Seven

Families

Leo Tolstoy states in the opening sentence of *Anna Karenina* that "Happy families are alike; every unhappy family is unhappy in its own way." Families in times of stress, difficulty, or unhappiness are interesting families. The interest lies in observing how family members react to difficulties and in noticing whether they grow from their circumstances or surrender to them. The films in this chapter, generally speaking, show unhappy families—families in pain or crisis. In compiling a list of films that focus on families, we have identified four essential attributes that often appear in these films:

1. Each film has a group of people who are united as a family, either through blood relationship or through friendship.

2. Conflicts result from the clash of the parents' values with their children's developing values, or from true dysfunction or abuse in the family.

3. Love and affection are either expressed between family members or are noticeably absent.

4. In films about family relationships, adolescents often come to realize for the first time that their parents are vulnerable human beings with their own problems and shortcomings.

Annotated List of Films

Information provided for each film is title, country (if other than the United States), director, year of release, MPAA rating, length, and language (if other than English). Films are in alphabetical order by title.

The Bicycle Thief (Italy, Vittorio De Sica, 1949, NR, 90 min., in Italian.)

A classic of postwar neorealism, *The Bicycle Thief* tells the story of Antonio, a poor laborer whose work depends on his having a bicycle. When the bicycle is stolen, the authorities refuse to take action, so he and his son search throughout Rome.

Breaking Away (Peter Yates, 1979, PG, 100 min.)

"The Cutters," a group of working-class high school graduates, find themselves at odds with their families and with the college kids in their Indiana town. They enter a bike race and learn to accept themselves as they "break away" from childhood and from their underdog self-images.

Brighton Beach Memoirs (Gene Saks, 1987, PG-13, 110 min.)

For annotation see Chapter Six.

Careful, He Might Hear You (Australia, Carl Schultz, 1983, PG, 116 min.)

Seven-year-old P. S. is the object of a custody battle waged by his two aunts in Australia of the 1930s. The story follows P. S.'s point of view as the aunts—unsuccessfully—try to keep the child from learning the details of their disagreement. Finally he is rescued by the father he has never met.

Clara's Heart (Robert Mulligan, 1988, PG-13, 108 min.)

A twelve-year-old boy's infant sister dies, throwing the family into turmoil. As his parents go through a divorce, the boy confides in Clara, their Jamaican housekeeper.

Crooklyn (Spike Lee, 1994, PG-13, 112 min.)

For annotation see Chapter Six.

Cross My Heart (France, Jacques Fansten, 1992, NR, 105 min., in French)

Young Martin's mother dies. When his friends find out, they help him conceal her death so that he won't have to go to an orphanage. As they unite to take care of him, Martin begins to thrive in school.

Fanny and Alexander (Sweden, Ingmar Bergman, 1983, R, 197 min., in Swedish.)

When their father dies, Fanny and Alexander's mother marries a stern Protestant minister. This autobiographical film, set in 1907, depicts one year in the life of the Ekdahl family as seen through the eyes of the two children.

The Great Santini (Lewis John Carlino, 1979, PG, 116 min.)

Based on the novel by Pat Conroy, this film focuses on the conflict between a domineering Marine father and his eighteen-year-old son. Several scenes powerfully depict the violence in this dysfunctional family. A secondary plot involves a friendship between the son and a simple-minded black man.

The Inkwell (Matty Rich, 1994, R, 112 min.)

For annotation see Chapter Six.

King of the Hill (Steven Soderberg, 1993, PG-13, 102 min.)

For annotation see Chapter Six.

Life Is a Long Quiet River (France, Etienne Chatiliez, 1987, NR, 89 min., in French.)

The Le Quesnoys are a refined upper-class family with well-behaved children; the Groseilles are a slovenly family with children who are streetwise thieves. The conflict—and comedy—begins when it is discovered that a disgruntled nurse switched babies at birth. The Le Quesnoys must cope with the fact that their daughter Bernadette is not really their child, while the Groseilles plan to become rich by selling Maurice back to his real family.

My Father's Glory/My Mother's Castle (France, Yves Robert, 1991, G/PG, 110 min./98 min.)

These two companion films, which take place in turn-of-the-century France, center around a bright young boy whose schoolteacher father takes his family on holiday to a village in Provence. In *My Father's Glory*, the boy falls in love with the countryside and never wants to leave, even when he must return home to prepare for national examinations. The sequel, *My Mother's Castle*, shows the family, which now spends every weekend at the summer house, taking a shortcut by trespassing through several neighboring estates in order to save hours of travel time. One of the estate owners apprehends them and then befriends the family, treating them like his special guests.

My Life as a Dog (Sweden, Lasse Hallström, 1987, NR, 101 min., in Swedish.)

When his mother becomes ill, a young boy is sent to live with relatives in a small Swedish village during the 1950s. There he meets a lively cast of village characters in this sensitive, funny, and heartwarming film. This is a great classroom film, but teachers should be alert to an anatomical reference in one of the opening scenes.

Ordinary People (Robert Redford, 1980, R, 123 min.)

Conrad Jarrett repeats his junior year in high school following several months in a mental hospital, where he has been after attempting suicide. With the help of a psychiatrist, Conrad comes to understand the source of his depression and feelings of worthlessness. Based on the novel by Judith Guest, this is a powerful film that won Academy Awards for Best Director, Best Supporting Actor, and Best Picture. (The R rating is for adult language.)

Peppermint Soda (France, Diane Kurys, 1977, NR, 97 min., in French.)

Anne and Frederique Weber, ages thirteen and fifteen, live in Paris with their divorced mother. This film chronicles a school year in which both girls struggle against the authority of an oppressive school and against their mother's (sometimes feeble) attempts to maintain control over her daughters. A highlight of the film is the often hilarious portrayal of the teachers in the private girls' school.

Rich in Love (Bruce Beresford, 1993, PG-13, 105 min.)

For annotation see Chapter Six.

A River Runs Through It (Robert Redford, 1992, PG, 123 min.)

A stern minister heads the Maclean family. The two sons are as different as Cain and Abel. Norman, the older son, follows the family's dream of college success, while Paul, the younger one, rebels with tragic results. Throughout the family's conflicts and reconciliations, the father and sons return to the activity that unites them all: fly-fishing for trout in a magnificent river.

Running on Empty (Sidney Lumet, 1988, PG-13, 116 min.)

High school senior Danny is a talented pianist and wants to go to Julliard. However, he lives with his parents and younger brother "underground," because his parents are wanted by the FBI for a politically motivated bombing fifteen years earlier. Danny has grown to accept the necessity of moving from town to town and taking another identity on a moment's notice, but when he falls in love with a girl and decides to pursue his interest in music, he knows he will have to choose between his dreams and his family. The strong portrayal of the closely knit family is noteworthy.

Sugar Cane Alley (Martinique, Euzhan Palcy, 1983, NR, 100 min., in French.)

José is a bright young boy growing up in the cane fields of Martinique. His grandmother recognizes his gifts and is determined that he become educated and leave Sugar Cane Alley and the hard life of the cane cutters. The special relationship between José and his grandmother is a highlight of this film.

This Is My Life (Nora Ephron, 1992, PG, 94 min.)

For annotation see Chapter Six.

Unstrung Heroes (Diane Keaton, 1995, PG, 94 min.)

Steven leads a comfortable and interesting life in the 1950s in Los Angeles with a doting mother, quirky-but-loving inventor father, and a darling little sister. When the mother develops a terminal illness, the boy runs away to live with his extremely eccentric uncles, who teach him about the importance of collecting kitschy junk, the magic of escaped balls, and his Jewish heritage, which his father has rejected. This is a lovely, sad movie about growing up, finding out who you are, and losing loved ones.

The War (John Avnet, 1995, PG-13, 126 min.)

Lydia and Stu's father has come home to Juliette, Mississippi, from fighting in Vietnam, but he is unable to find steady work. While their dad moves from job to job, his children spend the summer building a tree house and fighting with a family of ruffians who live in the town dump. This film vividly depicts the trials of growing up in poverty and the love among family members. The PG-13 rating is for language.

What's Eating Gilbert Grape (Lasse Hallström, 1993, PG-13, 118 min.)

The unconventional Grape family has more than its share of tribulations: a grotesquely overweight mother who hasn't left the house in years and a retarded eighteen-year-old son who is too old to be treated like a child and too immature to be trusted as an adult. Keeping the family together is oldest son, Gilbert, who both loves his family and is embarrassed by them. The scenes between the two brothers are particularly moving.

A World Apart (Chris Menges, 1988, PG, 114 min.)

Molly Roth is a white teenager living in Johannesburg, South Africa, in 1963. Her parents are active in the black Africans' struggle for independence from apartheid. When her father leaves suddenly to escape arrest and her mother risks her own freedom to continue the fight, Molly finds herself torn between love and loyalty to her parents and her own need for security.

The Essential Attributes of Films About Families and Family Relationships

What Constitutes a Family?

The families in this group of films include traditional, tight-knit "nuclear" families; families torn apart by divorce and death; and groups of people united by choice and love rather than by biology.

In this group of family films, the traditional nuclear family typically consists of both parents and some children, at least one of whom is an adolescent. The adolescent in the family plays a central role in the plot of the film. In *The Great Santini*, for example, the family consists of Bull Meachum; his wife, Lillian; and their four children; but the film concentrates on Ben and Mary Ann, the two older children, and their relationship with their father. The opening scene of *A World Apart* shows the home where Gus and Diana Roth live with their three daughters, but it quickly becomes clear that the older daughter, Molly, is the focal point of the film. The plot of *My Father's Glory* and *My Mother's Castle* involves the Pagnol family and their idyllic times in their vacation home in Provence, but we view the family through the eyes of the older son who would like to give up school altogether and live in the country.

Other families are fragmented—that is, they are missing or separated from an original family member and they suffer from the loss. The Jarrett family in *Ordinary People* has lost a son in a boating accident. In *Clara's Heart*, the family has lost an infant daughter and the parents are divorcing. When his mother becomes ill and cannot care for him, Ingemar (*My Life as a Dog*) is sent to live with relatives in a distant village. Martin (*Cross My Heart*) becomes an orphan when his mother dies.

Often, as a result of the loss, the families grow from and are enriched by the addition of people who adopt the family or become adopted by family members. When Molly Roth's father leaves the country and her mother is arrested (in *A World Apart*), their housekeeper, Elsie, and their grandmother care for Molly and her sisters. Clara, the Jamaican housekeeper in *Clara's Heart*, becomes a substitute mother to a boy whose own family is in turmoil. A group of his young friends adopt Martin (*Cross My Heart*) and help him hide the fact that he has been orphaned. Big-hearted villagers take in Ingemar (*My Life as a Dog*) and make him a part of their extended family.

Sometimes the families are groups of unrelated people. José and his grandmother (*Sugar Cane Alley*) are all that are left of their family, but they are clearly part of a larger family of their village on the island of Martinique. Aaron (*King of the Hill*) is virtually abandoned by his family, but he is looked after by other residents of the hotel he calls home. The Cutters, a group of working-class young men (*Breaking Away*) band together as a family against the college kids who make them feel inferior.

Family Conflicts

Conflicts in family films often result when adolescents test their developing values against the established values of their parents or their community. Anne and Frederique Weber (*Peppermint Soda*) pit their wills against both their mother and their teachers in their private girls' school. In *A River Runs Through It*, the conflict is between rebellious Paul Maclean and his father, a straight-laced Presbyterian minister. The values of Ben and Mary Ann Meachum (*The Great Santini*) conflict with the conservative views of their Marine father. In one scene, Mary Ann tries to divert her father's attention from the newspaper he is reading by facetiously telling him she has a boyfriend who is all the things he despises: a black, homosexual, pacifist midget. But in this film the conflict is more than one of values: the Meachum family is a dysfunctional family due, in large part, to the abusive Bull Meachum.

Other teenage protagonists also come from dysfunctional families. Gilbert Grape's family (*What's Eating Gilbert Grape*) is a mess: his mother is an obese recluse and his eighteen-year-old brother is mentally handicapped. Gilbert becomes the stabilizing force in his household and keeps the family together. Following the death of his brother, Conrad Jarrett (*Ordinary People*) is in many ways the sanest member of his family. After a suicide attempt and months of therapy with a caring psychiatrist, Conrad becomes whole again. The conflict arises because his parents, particularly his mother, have not grieved over their lost son and will not talk about their feelings with the son who survives.

The Expression of Love in Families

In films about family relationships, love and affection are an issue. Either they are expressed or the lack of their expression is painfully obvious. In *The War*, the father is openly affectionate with his two children, but not so with his wife, until the teenage daughter coaches her father to dance with her mother. In *Unstrung Heroes* Steven and his mother are very demonstrative in their affection, but the father tends to hold back. The film's final scene between the son and his father is a moving example of a family coming together to grieve over the loss of a loved one.

On the other hand, some families do not or cannot express affection. In *Careful, He Might Hear You*, the aunts never express any affection for their nephew. In *A World Apart*, Diana Roth is often brusque and businesslike with her daughters. When Conrad kisses his mother in one scene in *Ordinary People*, she does not respond at all, but stiffly endures her son's gesture of love.

Even in families where there is conflict and abuse, there are moments when the family members express their love for each other. Bull Meachum (*The Great Santini*) is an abusive father and husband, but the film makes it clear that he loves his family. Bull reveals his affection for his family on his son Ben's eighteenth birthday, when he gives Ben a Marine pilot's jacket and in a moving scene describes how proud he was the day Ben was born. In *The Inkwell*, Drew Tate has a strained relationship with his father. While Drew's mother is affectionate with him, Drew and his father avoid each other. The two weeks the family spends on Martha's Vineyard are therapeutic for both father and son. By the end of their vacation, they have spent time with each other, talked and listened to each other, and even hugged each other.

Adolescents See Their Parents as Human Beings

Adolescents in films often come to see their parents with new eyes and recognize, occasionally with embarrassment, their parents' failings. The recognition sometimes comes when teenagers see their parents through the eyes of other characters. In *King of the Hill* Aaron already has an inkling that his father is not a particularly good candle salesman and he knows from first-hand experience that his father is not adequately providing for his family. But Aaron is not embarrassed by his father until he is riding in a car with a friend from school and the car passes his father who is sitting dejectedly on some steps next to his box of candles. His friend's mother points to Aaron's father and laughingly comments, "That man is selling candles that won't even light." Mortified, Aaron does not admit that he knows the man.

Other times, even though the adults in their lives try to project a facade of stability, adolescents have first-hand glimpses of their parents at their most vulnerable. Lucille (*Rich in Love*) observes the misery her father experiences when his wife leaves him. Troy Carmichael and her brothers (*Crooklyn*) see their father's vulnerable side when their mother kicks him out of the house after a violent family quarrel. Molly Roth (*A World Apart*) reads a note her mother wrote secretly in a Bible and learns that her mother attempted suicide while in prison. Molly reacts with anger, accusing her mother of trying to abandon her daughters. The argument that ensues is resolved when Molly realizes how torn her mother is between her work to end apartheid and her role as a mother.

Writing Assignments

1. Choose one film that contains all the essential attributes of films about families. Write an analytical essay in which you explain how that film treats the essential attributes.

2. Watch two films with very different families—an abusive or dysfunctional situation (such as *The Great Santini* or *Ordinary People*) and a more openly loving family (*The Inkwell, Brighton Beach Memoirs,* or *Running on Empty*). In an essay compare and contrast the various ways family love is expressed in the two films.

3. Watch a film about a "non-nuclear" family (*Clara's Heart, Sugar Cane Alley,* or *My Life as a Dog*). Using evidence from the film, write an essay that answers the question: What are the characteristics of a family?

4. Write a job description for a parent. Watch a film about a family and then, based on your job description, write a "performance evaluation" of one or more of the parents in that film.

5. Many films on the theme of family relationships show the point of view of the children in the family. Choose a film about families that emphasizes the child's point of view. Then, take the point of view of one of the adults in the film and write several journal entries from that character's point of view.

6. Write a paper describing your family—not just your immediate family, your blood relations, but all the people you're bound to by love and affection.

7. (a) If you could spend the summer with one of the families in these films, which family would you choose? Write a letter to the parents of the family asking to join them for a summer. Tell them why you admire them as a family. (b) Identify the family with which you would *least* like to spend time. Imagine that they have invited you to spend the summer with them. Write a letter to the parents in which you decline the invitation. Tell them why you would *not* like to be a member of their family—even for the summer.

8. Watch a film about a dysfunctional family. Then choose a character and write a letter to "Dear Abby" from that character's point of view, asking for advice. Write the response letter the character would receive from Abby.

9. Compare and contrast the father-son relationships in the film *The Great Santini* and in Chris Crutcher's novel *The Crazy Horse Electric Game*.

10. (a) Watch either *Clara's Heart* or *Ordinary People* and read Will Weaver's novel *Striking Out*. Compare and contrast how families are affected by the death of a child. (b) Watch either *This Is My Life, Rich in Love, A World Apart,* or *Peppermint Soda* and read Joyce Sweeney's novel *The Tiger Orchard*. Compare and contrast the ways families cope with a missing parent.

Chapter Eight

Belonging

Adolescents want to belong and be like everyone else, but they also want to be unique individuals. As they try to find their place in the social realm, they judge themselves against their peers. They worry: Am I normal? Am I good enough? Am I smart enough? Am I pretty enough? Do I fit in?

The need to belong is not unique to adolescents, but by the time they are adults, most people have made accommodations and have either found ways to belong or have developed coping skills to handle not belonging. Adolescents are struggling to gain acceptance and, for many of them, this struggle consumes and drives their teenage years.

We have identified three essential attributes that appear in films about belonging.

1. Tension exists between an individual and a group.

2. The plot is often driven by what the individual does to be accepted by the group or by the protagonist's active attempts to remain separate.

3. In order to resolve the conflict, someone—either the individual or the group—must change or make accommodations.

Annotated List of Films

Information provided for each film is title, country (if other than the United States), director, year of release, MPAA rating, length, and language (if other than English). Films are in alphabetical order by title.

Addams Family Values (Barry Sonnenfeld, 1993, PG-13, 94 min.)

One of the subplots of this hilarious film involves sending Pugsley and Wednesday, the Addams' adolescent children, to a summer camp where almost all of the campers are white, blond, and suburban. Needless to say, the Addams children don't fit in. They band together with the other misfits—Jewish, black, Asian, or just plain nerdy—to stage a rebellion.

Angus (Patrick Read Johnson, 1995, PG-13, 87 min.)

In this film, based on a short story by Chris Crutcher, Angus Bethune is a high school freshman who is a member of the junior varsity football team and a gifted science student. He is also extremely overweight. When—as a joke—Angus is elected king of the winter dance, he must dance with the girl whom he has secretly loved for years. Angus is terrified of embarrassing himself in front of the school and in front of this young woman. In dealing with this crisis, Angus is supported by his mother, his grandfather, and his best friend. This film takes a sensitive look at the issue of coming to terms with one's identity.

Au Revoir les Enfants (France, Louis Malle, 1987, PG, 104 min., in French.)

During World War II, two French schoolboys in a Catholic boarding school become friends. The conflict arises when it becomes apparent that one of the boys is a Jewish student who is being hidden in the school to protect him from the Nazis. Noteworthy in this film are the strong friendship between Jean and Julien, and the character of the priest who works to save Jewish children.

Benny & Joon (Jeremiah S. Chechik, 1993, PG, 98 min.)

Benny runs a garage and tries to keep up with his mentally disturbed sister, Joon, who has a history of setting fires. When Benny wins Sam, the cousin of a friend, in a poker game, Joon finds a soul mate in this eccentric young man. This film shows the love between the brother and sister, Benny's desperation in dealing with his difficult sister, and the transforming power of love.

Breaking Away (Peter Yates, 1979, PG, 100 min.)

For annotation see Chapter Seven.

Clueless (Amy Heckerling, 1995, PG-13, 97 min.)

Cher Horowitz has it all. Her father is a successful lawyer who provides well for his daughter and she is a member of the popular crowd at her high school. Early in the movie, her stepbrother Josh accuses Cher of being a superficial valley girl, and it's true that she is very concerned with clothes, parties, and boyfriends. As the film progresses, however, Cher is revealed to be much more. She takes care of her father and is concerned about his eating habits, and she coaches a new (and unattractive) student at her high school in ways to dress and attract guys. Even Josh comes to recognize a depth in Cher he had not thought was present. (*Clueless* is loosely based on the novel *Emma* by Jane Austen.)

Dark Horse (David Hemmings, 1992, PG, 95 min.)

For annotation see Chapter Six.

Europa, Europa (Germany, Agnieszka Holland, 1991, R, 115 min., in German.)

Solomon Perel is a teenage German Jew. When his sister is killed by Nazis in 1938, the family moves to Poland, beginning a series of incredible events for young Solly. He escapes to Russia, living for a time in a Communist orphanage. He is recaptured by the Nazis and eventually ends up in a training school for elite members of the Hitler Youth. Solly survives by keeping his Jewish identity secret—not an easy task in the environment of the school. This is a compelling story, made all the more so because it is true. (The R rating is for nudity and violence.)

Housekeeping (Bill Forsyth, 1988, PG, 112 min.)

Two orphaned sisters come into the custody of their free-spirited aunt in the 1950s. Her lack of responsibility charms one of them and alienates the other, who wants to go to school and be like everyone else.

The Inkwell (Matty Rich, 1994, R, 112 min.)

For annotation see Chapter Six.

La Boum (France, Claude Pinoteau, 1980, NR, 100 min.)

When thirteen-year-old Vic's family moves to a new town, her life is thrown into upheaval. First she must figure out how to make friends in her new surroundings, then how to navigate the "boums" (big weekend parties) given by her new friends. Meanwhile her parents are having problems of their own.

Lantern Hill (Kevin Sullivan, 1989, NR, 110 min.)

Jane Stuart is twelve years old in 1935 when her mother's illness forces her to live with a houseful of cold, snooty relatives in Toronto. Jane's misery is compounded when the father she has always believed dead sends for her to visit him at his home on Prince Edward Island. Arriving in the small community, Jane discovers that her father is suspected of murder. She learns the truth and comes to understand her father, helped in part by a local woman with special powers.

Let Him Have It (Great Britain, Peter Medak, 1991, R, 115 min.)

Set in London in the 1950s, this film is based on a true story that was responsible for changes in England's death penalty. Because nineteen-year-old Derek Bentley is slow witted and a bit too trusting of his teenage friends, he gets involved with a group of thieves who model themselves on Hollywood gangsters. On one burglary, his younger friend Chris pulls a gun on a policeman, who asks him to hand it over. Derek says, "Let him have it, Chris," and the boy shoots and kills the policeman. Derek faces trial for murder as an adult while Chris is remanded to juvenile court. The outcome of the trial turns on the interpretation of Derek's statement: Was he encouraging the murder or telling Chris to hand over the gun? Although the film is slow going in the beginning, the last part of the film (the trial and its aftermath) is riveting and provides an excellent case study for debates on capital punishment.

Lucas (David Seltzer, 1986, PG-13, 100 min.)

Lucas, a gifted fourteen-year-old, is the high school nerd. When a new girl arrives in town, she and Lucas become friends. Lucas is devastated when she tries out for cheerleader and begins to ignore him for the more popular kids at school. He tries to get her attention by trying out for the football team. This film is a sensitive look at the issues of popularity and belonging.

Mask (Peter Bogdanovich, 1985, PG-13, 120 min.)

Rocky Dennis is the ultimate outsider, a teenager so facially disfigured by lionitis that it's difficult for other people even to look at him. His main support is his mother, who in spite of her biker lifestyle loves him fiercely.

My Bodyguard (Tony Bill, 1980, PG, 96 min.)

Clifford Peache is a high school sophomore who has transferred to a new school. As the new kid, he experiences rejection and teenage terrorism. In seeking a bodyguard, Clifford learns the dark truth about Ricky Linderman, an alleged "mass murderer." Cliff and his eccentric grandmother reach out to Ricky and, in accepting Ricky, Cliff learns about his own strength.

Powder (Victor Salva, 1995, PG-13, 112 min.)

Jeremy Reed is an extremely gifted albino child who has grown up in his grandparents' basement. When the grandfather dies, Jeremy is taken to the state youth home, where his other extraordinary powers soon surface. He is capable of generating a powerful electrical energy field as well as listening so closely to people that he can hear their thoughts, feelings, and memories. Needless to say, Jeremy has problems connecting with his fellow students and regularly experiences being misunderstood. However, this parable of the "mysterious stranger" has lessons about people's fear of connecting with one another, about love and reconciliation, and about death and resurrection. The film is ambiguous enough to allow a variety of interpretations (is Jeremy an outsider, a freak, a genius, an angel, or a messiah?), which should appeal to high school students.

Rebel Without a Cause (Nicholas Ray, 1955, NR, 111 min.)

Jim Stark is a high school student who doesn't understand his parents and doesn't feel that his parents understand him. His life becomes complicated when he moves to a new town and tries very hard but fails to fit in with the "in" group at the high school. Jim does make friends with two lonely teenagers and the three young people stand together against the rest of the world. Even though this film is more than forty years old, it still speaks to adolescents about alienation and the need to belong.

School Ties (Robert Mandel, 1992, PG-13, 110 min.)

David Greene, an excellent football player from a working-class neighborhood, is recruited by a prestigious prep school in the 1950s. All goes well until his fellow students find out he's Jewish and begin a campaign of intimidation and harassment.

Welcome Home, Roxy Carmichael (**Jim Abrahams, 1990,**
PG-13, 98 min.)

Roxy Carmichael left her small town in Ohio, her teenaged boy-friend, and her baby sixteen years ago to go to Hollywood. Now she's coming home to a town celebration in her honor. A high school girl, convinced that she is the baby Roxy left behind, prepares to meet her mother. This film presents an interesting study of a teenager's need to belong.

The Essential Attributes of Films About Belonging

Individuals in Conflict with Groups

In films about belonging, an adolescent typically tries to join a group, but ends up being rejected by the group. The reason for the group's rejection of the individual is simple: the individual is different from the group in some way. Sometimes the individual is a new kid in town. Clifford Peache (*My Bodyguard*) is terrorized in his new school until he hires one of the toughest kids as a bodyguard. After moving from Los Angeles, Allie (*Dark Horse*) has trouble fitting in and adjusting to life in a small town.

Individuals may be different physically, sometimes grotesquely so: Jeremy Reed (*Powder*) is albino; Rocky Dennis (*Mask*) suffers from lionitis, a disease that has left his face horribly deformed. Other individuals are rejected because of a mental disorder or retardation. In *Benny & Joon*, Joon's schizophrenia causes her to behave in ways that single her out and embarrass her brother. Derek Bentley (*Let Him Have It*) is mildly retarded and has trouble fitting in with his peers. He is accepted by a gang of thieves only because he participates in their burglaries.

In films about belonging, a group typically rejects an individual because something about the individual offends the values of the group. The group may value beauty or popularity—in short, people like themselves. In *School Ties*, the popular group of athletes accepts David until they learn that he is Jewish. Then he is rejected and harassed. In *Breaking Away*, the college students reject the Cutters for their working-class status. In *Lucas*, the protagonist is gifted but nerdy, and he accepts his role as outcast. His life changes when a new girl arrives in town and befriends him, and Lucas sets out to join the group that values looks and athletic prowess over academic success.

Sometimes protagonists have secrets that keep them out of the group or make them different in some way. In *Europa, Europa*, Solomon Perel's secret is that he is Jewish. His problem arises not in trying to belong (he's very good at that), but in keeping those who have accepted him from finding out his secret. Jean Bonnet is also Jewish and is keeping his religion a secret in *Au Revoir les Enfants*.

Seeking Acceptance

The plot of these films is often driven by the attempts of the individual to gain the acceptance of the group. Jim Stark (*Rebel Without a Cause*) participates in "chickie" races to gain acceptance by the popular kids in his new high school. In order to keep his girlfriend, Lucas tries out for the football team and sets himself up for ridicule. In *My Bodyguard*, Clifford Peache seeks protection and acceptance by hiring Ricky Linderman to be his bodyguard. Vic (*La Boum*) tries to fit in by learning the protocol associated with the weekend parties given by her new friends.

Sometimes the individual does not really try to be accepted by the group. Jeremy Reed (*Powder*) is perfectly self-sufficient (or so he believes) and does not seek acceptance, but because of his grotesque appearance and his special powers, his fellow students torment him. Jean and Julien (*Au Revoir les Enfants*) are two friends in a French boarding school who are different from the other boys because they are readers and thinkers. The two do not try to be like the other boys in the school. In *Breaking Away*, the Cutters are not accepted by the college students, but they seem to have a group pride and do not seek to belong to the higher status group.

Making Accommodations

Groups do not tolerate anyone who is different. In films about belonging, when adolescents cease being outcasts and are accepted by a group, one of two events has occurred: either the individual or the group has made accommodations.

Belonging to the group is so important to adolescents that they will try to change themselves drastically to belong. Lucas has always claimed to hate athletes, but he tries out for the football team. In *Dark Horse*, Allie goes so far as to break the law in order to ingratiate herself with a group of students in her new school. In *Europa, Europa*, Solly constantly adjusts to his new environment, doing whatever is necessary in order to survive—posing as a Communist, a Nazi, and a Gentile, and even mutilating himself.

adam's mark.
hotels & resorts

Gunther Kress – book on pix + comp

Sometimes members of the group reach out to the outsiders and draw them into the group. Cher and Dionne (*Clueless*) are members of the popular group at their high school. They befriend a new girl whom they see as "clueless," giving her a make-over and tutoring her in how to behave in order to attract a popular boyfriend. Judy (*Rebel Without a Cause*) is a member of the popular group who reaches out to Jim Stark and introduces him to other group members. In *Powder*, a popular girl in Jeremy's class is attracted by his powers of empathy and befriends him, and in so doing, she angers her father who cannot tolerate his daughter making friends with a freak.

Sometimes the group recognizes special qualities in the outsider and comes to accept that individual. Rocky Dennis (*Mask*) is horribly disfigured. When he enrolls in his new school, the other students are repulsed by him, but Rocky understands and is patient. As time passes, his fellow students get to know him, and by the end of the school year he is an accepted and valued member of the class.

Suggested Writing Assignments

1. Take the three essential attributes for films dealing with belonging and apply them to a film from the list. Write an analytical essay in which you explain how the film exemplifies the attributes.

2. Most of the groups to which the protagonists want to belong have stated or unstated rules or standards for belonging. Watch one film and make a list of all the requirements for belonging to the group. Design an "application form" for belonging to this group. Then fill out the form as if you are the protagonist.

3. Watch *Addams Family Values* and write an essay on how this film is a satire of films on belonging.

4. Write a personal narrative on "A Time I Wanted to Belong" or "A Time I Kept Someone Else from Belonging."

5. Watch a film on belonging and—assuming that the film does not have a theme song—choose a popular song that would make a good theme song for the film. Write a letter to the film's director, suggesting that he or she use the song in the film. Provide reasons the song would be a good match for the film.

6. Compare S. E. Hinton's novel *The Outsiders* or Richard Peck's *Remembering the Good Times* with *Rebel Without a Cause* or *Breaking Away*. In an essay, answer the question: What motivates people to belong? Cite examples from the book and film.

7. Sometimes concerns about belonging arise when a teenager moves from one environment to another. Compare and contrast S. E. Hinton's *Taming the Star Runner* and *Dark Horse*. Use the essential attributes for films about belonging to structure your analysis.

8. In many books and films about outsiders, the protagonist eventually chooses not to belong—to remain an outsider. Choose a novel such as Brock Cole's *The Goats*, Chris Crutcher's *Staying Fat for Sarah Byrnes*, or Robert Cormier's *The Chocolate War* and a film such as *School Ties*, *Powder*, or *Welcome Home, Roxy Carmichael*. Compare and contrast the novel and the film as to why the protagonists choose to remain outsiders.

Chapter Nine

Dreams and Quests

Adolescents spend their teenage years getting ready for the rest of their lives. They are getting ready for high school, college, a career, or marriage and a family. They set goals and have dreams for their futures. They search for ways to live, to be adults, to make it on their own, to make sense of the world around them. Some films about dreamers have the protagonist engage in a literal journey or quest for meaning.

We have identified five essential attributes found in films about dreams and quests:

1. The protagonist has a dream, strives for a particular goal, or seeks the object of a quest.

2. Obstacles stand in the way of the dream and opportunities open up for the protagonist.

3. Sometimes protagonists lose heart or get discouraged and someone else has to hold onto the dream for them. In the case of a quest, sometimes the journey is directed or guided by a wiser, older person.

4. At the beginning of the story, the protagonists are all insufficient to the task and have to develop an aspect of their character in order to attain the goal or fulfill the quest.

5. The protagonists attain the dream or they do not—either way, they learn something valuable.

Annotated List of Films

Information provided for each film is title, country (if other than the United States), director, year of release, MPAA rating, length, and language (if other than English). Films are in alphabetical order by title.

American Graffiti (George Lucas, 1973, PG, 112 min.)

On the night before Steve and Curt are to leave for college in 1962, they spend time with their friends John and Terry, riding around to various hangouts, going to a school dance, meeting new girls, witnessing a drag race, and so forth. This slice of 1960s life shows both Steve and Curt examining their priorities as they choose between home and college, between safety and the unknown. The nonstop rock and roll soundtrack comments on the action.

The Basketball Diaries (Scott Kalvert, 1995, R, 102 min.)

Based on poet Jim Carroll's teenage diaries detailing his experiences with drugs, this film's graphic depiction of crime, sex, and drug use will limit its classroom use. However, there are some powerful scenes—particularly one horrific drug withdrawal sequence and several scenes between Jim and his mother—that show the cost of drug abuse to this gifted ball player and poet. The ending of the film is hopeful: Jim gets free of drugs in prison and becomes a successful poet.

Boyz N the Hood (John Singleton, 1991, R, 112 min.)

This critically acclaimed film by first-time director John Singleton (twenty-five years old at the time he wrote and directed it) tells the story of three friends growing up in south central Los Angeles: Doughboy, a drug dealer; his brother, Ricky, bound for college on a football scholarship; and Tre, the focal character, longing to make something of his life but not immune to his surroundings. Particularly moving is the strong relationship between Tre and his father (appropriately named Furious Styles). The film is often bleak and violent, but there is hope. The world of the film is undeniably real. (The R rating is probably the result of the language and violence.)

Chariots of Fire (England, Hugh Hudson, 1981, PG, 123 min.)

Set at the 1924 Olympics, this film is the true story of English runners Eric Liddell and Harold Abrahams, and the decision of conscience that one of them must make.

Cooley High (Michael A. Schultz, 1975, PG, 107 min.)

Preach and Cochise are two African American teenagers living in Chicago in the early 1960s. They both attend Cooley Vocational High School, but most of the film follows Preach and Cochise's lives away from school as they walk the streets of Chicago, attend parties, and even run afoul of the law. Both of these young men have dreams: Preach wants to be a writer and Cochise wants to go to college. (The PG rating for this film is misleading, because the film contains some strong language and one explicit sexual scene.)

The Cure (1995, Peter Horton, PG-13, 99 min.)

Eric befriends Dexter, his eleven-year-old neighbor who has AIDS. Determined to find a cure so his friend won't die, Eric first designs a series of "treatments"—boiling and drinking an assortment of plants. Next, the boys read in a tabloid of a Louisiana doctor who claims to have found a cure in the bayous, so they set out on a raft down the Mississippi. In one memorable scene, Eric stands up to a group of bullies who harass the boys for being "faggots." This poignant, touching film contains accurate information about the transmission of AIDS and deals with bigotry.

December (Gabe Torres, 1991, PG, 92 min.)

A group of prep school boys reacts to the news of the bombing of Pearl Harbor. This film takes place in less than one day as the boys decide whether they will stay at school or enlist to fight in the war. A secondary plot concerns a censorship issue involving *Johnny Got His Gun*.

El Norte (Gregory Nava, 1983, R, 139 min., in English and Spanish.)

This independent American film tells the story of a teenage brother and sister who journey from their native Guatemala through Mexico and (illegally) enter the United States. Life in California is alien and confusing as they try to find work, learn English, and avoid being deported.

Fame (Alan Parker, 1980, R, 133 min.)

We follow a group of diverse and talented students from the time they enter ninth grade in New York City's High School of the Performing Arts until their graduation four years later. Some achieve their dreams, some are disappointed, and some fall tragically by the wayside. The movie has brilliant individual monologues and scenes, as well as contrived and unrealistic musical numbers. Still, the finale ("I Sing the Body Electric") is irresistible.

The Gods Must Be Crazy (Botswana, Jamie Uys, 1981, PG, 108 min.)

When a Coke bottle falls from the sky, it brings turmoil to a peaceful tribe of Bushmen. The leaders of the tribe commission one of its members to take the evil object to the edge of the world and give it back to the gods. Though technically not an adolescent, the protagonist undertakes a quest that is both poignant and comical.

Hoop Dreams (Steve James, 1994, PG-13, 176 min.)

When they enter the ninth grade, Arthur Agee and William Gates have a dream: to play professional basketball like their hero and fellow Chicagoan Isiah Thomas. This documentary film follows these two young men for their entire high school career and into college as they pursue their dreams. Along the way we meet coaches, friends, and family members who provide both inspiration and roadblocks to the two young men. The film vividly demonstrates that Arthur and William's dream is one that can be realized by only a few players, and that in order to achieve their goal they must stay focused and work extraordinarily hard.

Hoosiers (David Anspaugh, 1986, PG, 114 min.)

A basketball coach with a mysterious past arrives in a small town in Indiana to take over the high school basketball team. His coaching techniques irritate the parents, but his success with the team and with the individual players makes this a heartwarming film.

The Journey of Natty Gann (Jeremy Kagan, 1985, PG, 101 min.)

In 1935, teenager Natty Gann is separated from her father when he leaves Chicago suddenly for a job in Washington state. When she runs afoul of the landlady, Natty sets out to find her father by "riding the rails" west. Along the way she is befriended by a wolf and meets a variety of drifters.

The Loneliness of the Long Distance Runner (Great Britain, Tony Richardson, 1962, NR, 104 min.)

A juvenile delinquent is sentenced to time in a borstal, where, due to progressive ideas about rehabilitation, he is allowed to train as a long-distance runner. Running brings him great satisfaction and a feeling of freedom, but during a crucial track meet with a posh private school, he realizes that his success justifies the social system he hates so much.

Musashi Miyamoto (Samurai I) (Japan, Hiroshi Inaga-ki, 1954, NR, 92 min., in Japanese.)

In the first film of the *Samurai Trilogy*, Takezo (later to become the famous samurai Musashi Miyamoto) is young, wild, and foolish. Taken in hand by a Buddhist priest who first teaches him discipline and then the way of the samurai, Takezo begins the training that eventually makes him one of the most respected men in medieval Japan.

My Brilliant Career (Australia, Gillian Armstrong, 1979, G, 102 min.)

For annotation see Chapter Six.

The Nasty Girl (Germany, Michael Verhoeven, 1990, PG-13, 94 min.)

Sonya Rosenberger narrates her life story, focusing on her attempt as a high school student to research and write an essay on "My Hometown During the Third Reich." At first, no one will talk to her or give her access to any documents, forcing her to sue the town. It seems that several upstanding citizens have not been honest about their actions regarding the Nazis.

Pathfinder (Norway, Nils Gaup, 1988, NR, 88 min., in Lappish.)

Set in Lapland in the tenth or eleventh century, this film tells the story of Aigin, a young man who witnesses his family's murder by marauding thieves. He tries to warn a nearby village, but he is captured and forced to become the pathfinder for the thieves. This is truly a foreign film—in time, in location, and in language—but the story is a compelling one that demonstrates the sources of legends and the power of myth.

Pelle the Conqueror (Sweden, Bille August, 1988, PG-13, 140 min., in Swedish and Danish.)

In the late nineteenth century, young Pelle leaves his native Sweden with his father for a life of hard work on a farm in Denmark. While he adapts to farm life, his eyes are opened to his father's weaknesses, and he is determined to realize his dream to be free and to conquer the world.

Rudy (David Anspaugh, 1993, PG, 112 min.)

In this film based on a true story, Rudy Ruettiger has a dream to play football at Notre Dame. The problem is that Rudy doesn't have the grades to attend Notre Dame and his small size makes playing college football next to impossible. After high school, Rudy follows his father and brothers to work in the steel mill of his home town of Gary, Indiana; but when his best friend dies in an accident at the mill, Rudy sets off to South Bend to try to enroll in Notre Dame. With the help of people who are impressed with his determination and with hard work on his part, Rudy is finally accepted at Notre Dame and becomes a walk-on for the football team. This film demonstrates the importance of dreams and how dreams can come true when people work hard enough to achieve them.

Running on Empty (Sidney Lumet, 1988, PG-13, 116 min.)

For annotation see Chapter Seven.

Searching for Bobby Fischer (Steven Zaillian, 1993, PG, 111 min.)

Josh is a seven-year-old who demonstrates an amazing gift for chess. At first, his parents try to dissuade him from taking the game seriously, but when it becomes clear that Josh has the potential to become a very successful player (the next Bobby Fischer, in fact), his parents begin to push him to practice and succeed at the game. Josh is not an adolescent, but adolescents will relate both to the dream Josh has to be a world-class chess player and to his struggle with his parents over ownership of the dream.

Stand and Deliver (Ramon Menendez, 1988, PG, 105 min.)

A high school teacher achieves the impossible when he takes a group of low-achieving Hispanic high school students and prepares them for the Advanced Placement Test in calculus.

Stand by Me (Rob Reiner, 1986, R, 87 min.)

Four twelve-year-old friends set off from their Oregon town on a two-day journey in search of the body of a missing teenager. Along the way they discover friendship, their own strength, and the meaning of death.

Wild Hearts Can't Be Broken (Steve Miner, 1991, G, 89 min.)

This is the true story of Sonora Webster, the girl who rode the diving horses in Atlantic City in the 1930s. Sonora is a strong female protagonist, who persists in achieving something significant when the adults in her life try to discourage her.

The Essential Attributes of Films About Dreams and Quests

Dreamers and Dreams

In general, the adolescent protagonists in these films stand on the brink of adulthood and imagine a future worth striving for. For some, the future is a question of what to do after high school. Steve and Curt (*American Graffiti*) face a decision about whether to leave for college on the next day. Danny (*Running on Empty*) dreams of going to Julliard to study piano. The students in *December* wrestle with the decision of whether to join the army or stay in school. The students at the performing arts high school in *Fame* dream of careers as dancers, actors, and musicians. Jim (*The Basketball Diaries*) and Sybilla (*My Brilliant Career*) want to be writers.

A number of the films in this group feature adolescent athletes whose dream is to be so excellent at their sport that they will get a scholarship (*Boyz N the Hood*), play on a college team (*Rudy*), finish first in a race (*The Loneliness of the Long Distance Runner*), win a championship game (*Hoosiers*), win an Olympic gold medal (*Chariots of Fire*), or be drafted by the pros (*Hoop Dreams*). Young Josh's parents want him to play chess like Bobby Fischer (*Searching for Bobby Fischer*) and Sonora (*Wild Hearts Can't Be Broken*) wants to excel at a seemingly impossible task: to ride a horse that dives from a platform into a tank of water.

Other dreams and quests focus less on a career but more on personal goals. Natty Gann wants to find her father. The brother and sister in *El Norte* want to make it to America and, once there, achieve the American Dream. The students in *Stand and Deliver* want to prove that they are capable of academic success. Eric and Dexter seek a cure for AIDS (*The Cure*). Aigin (*Pathfinder*) seeks revenge for his family's death. Takezo (*Musashi Miyamoto*) embarks on the path of training as a samurai in order to be powerful and respected.

Obstacles and Opportunities

The plot in these films is often driven by a series of obstacles that the protagonist must overcome in order to achieve the dream or fulfill the quest. The obstacles may be a personal characteristic of the hero that is at least an inconvenience (Natty Gann's gender or Eric Liddell's devout Christianity in *Chariots of Fire*) or sometimes a serious shortcoming (Rudy's size or Jim's drug addiction in *The Basketball Diaries*). Sometimes the obstacle is a characteristic of the society that surrounds the protagonist: anti-Semitism in *Chariots of Fire*, the townspeople's urge to bury their Nazi past in *The Nasty Girl*, and the violence and despair of the ghetto in *Boyz N the Hood* and *Hoop Dreams*.

In nearly every film, the protagonist also benefits from opportunities—good fortune—along the journey. In many cases, the protagonist's main source of support is a family member: the father's obvious love for his son in *Boyz N the Hood*, a loving mother and father willing to make sacrifices so their son can pursue his dream in *Running on Empty*, and the coaches and family members in *Hoop Dreams*.

Some characters succeed because they create their own opportunities. For example, several of the kids in *Fame* pursue auditions outside the school, the brother and sister in *El Norte* run away from their village to journey to America, and Sybilla (in *My Brilliant Career*) trains as a teacher in order to pursue her dream of being a writer.

Often the main character is in just the right place at the right time. Curt (*American Graffiti*) meets the real Wolfman Jack and sees a vision of the perfect woman, who actually calls him on the phone. These twin epiphanies allow him to complete his high school years and step powerfully into his future. In *December*, the young men are of the appropriate age to join the army at the historic moment of the bombing of Pearl Harbor.

Dream Keepers and Guides

When the dreamer or seeker gets discouraged, often another character will hold onto the dream until the protagonist can take it up again. These dream keepers are often teachers, coaches, priests, and parents. The strong coach in *Hoosiers* first has to create the dream for the members of his basketball team and then train them in the skills they will need to make the journey to the state championship. Along the way, the coach is the one with the constant vision, even when the players see no possibility of success. In *The Basketball Diaries*, Jim is rescued by an older, recovered addict, who stays with him through the horrors of withdrawal. Furious Styles, the father in *Boyz N the Hood*, keeps reminding his son of the goal, sometimes protecting him with harsh discipline. The priest in *Musashi Miyamoto* goes so far as to lock Takezo in an attic as part of his training.

Developing Character to Achieve the Goal

In pursuing the dream, the protagonist often has to face personal deficiencies and then develop the necessary traits to achieve the dream or continue the quest. Rudy wants to play football for Notre Dame more than anything else, but at first he doesn't have the grades to get into the university, so he persists in taking courses at a junior college. Next he has to deal with the fact that he's too small to be effective on the team. Again he persists, taking on any job the coaches ask him to do. Finally, his determination and hard work pay off. Similarly, Takezo (*Musashi Miyamoto*) must overcome his rebellious nature and develop the strength and peace of mind required to be a samurai. He does this by surrendering to the teachings of a Buddhist priest. In the beginning of *Hoosiers*, some of the players actually have strong skills individually, but they do not play as a team. In order to become a championship team, they have to go back and relearn the fundamentals of passing, assisting, and defense.

The high school students in *American Graffiti* and *December* have to consider their options and make a choice between two divergent paths. The boys in *December* must weigh their values—such as patriotism, pacifism, and personal safety—against their expectation that war will be an adventure like no other. Curt (*American Graffiti*) has to give up his adolescent illusions (represented by Wolfman Jack and the girl in the Thunderbird) in order to take responsibility for his career.

Achieving the Dream

The films in this group usually end with the protagonist achieving the dream or the object of the quest. Natty finds her father, Rudy gets to play in an important game, the small town team wins the state championship, Jim publishes his poetry, and Takezo becomes a samurai. Such conclusions are triumphant and joyous, with appropriate celebration and expressions of gratitude.

Occasionally the conclusion is ambiguous or bittersweet. In *The Loneliness of the Long Distance Runner*, Colin is clearly the best runner in the race, but he stops short of the finish line in order to defy the officials of the penal system, thereby consigning himself to more months in the reformatory. In *Fame*, some students succeed brilliantly, while others meet defeat. A coda to *American Graffiti* tells us the futures of the main characters, ranging from satisfying to disappointing and tragic. At the end of *Running on Empty*, Danny has the opportunity to pursue his dream of being a classical pianist, but he can no longer live with his family.

Achieving the goal may provide the fulfillment the protagonists want, but sometimes the dream is hollow—they achieve the goal but at too great a cost, or they find that the goal is not really what they wanted. Such is the case with the boys in *Stand By Me*, who find the object of their search, but in doing so they have to face their own fears and failures. The brother and sister in *El Norte* do get to America, but life for illegal immigrants in California is hard and they aren't equipped to succeed.

In a few of these films, the protagonists fail to achieve their dreams, at least within the time span of the film. In both *Cooley High* and *Boyz N the Hood*, one of the main characters is murdered, and no one seems to learn anything from the tragedy. In *The Cure*, Eric doesn't find a cure for AIDS in time to save Dexter, but he comes to an understanding about friendship and the importance of being fully alive.

Writing Assignments

1. Watch one of the films about dreams or quests and analyze the film using the five essential attributes as a framework for discussion.

2. After watching several films dealing with dreams, select the protagonist that most inspires you. Write a letter to the screenwriter or director expressing your admiration for the character's accomplishments and how the character has inspired you to strive toward your goals and dreams.

3. After watching *Musashi Miyamoto*, conduct research on bushido, the code of behavior of the samurai. In a persuasive essay, describe the characteristics of a samurai and evaluate Takezo on his readiness to be a samurai. You might frame your essay as a report to the Shogun.

4. Write your own dream history. What did you dream of becoming when you were less than five years old? Between the ages of five and eleven? Twelve and now? What is your current dream? What obstacles and opportunities do you see before you? Who plays the role of dream keeper or guide in your life?

5. Compare the documentary *Hoop Dreams* with one of the fiction films about young athletes: *Rudy*, *Hoosiers*, *Chariots of Fire*, or *The Loneliness of the Long Distance Runner*. What conclusions can you draw about athletic goals as dreams?

6. Read a novel and compare it to one of the films about dreams and quests. Use the essential attributes to structure your comparison. Consider these pairs: *Running on Empty* and Suzanne Newton's *I Will Call It Georgie's Blues*, *Stand by Me* and Julian Thompson's *Band of Angels*, *Pathfinder* and Robert Cormier's *I Am the Cheese*, and *Hoop Dreams* and Walter Dean Myers' *Hoops*.

Chapter Ten

Love and Romance

Teenagers wallow in love. They listen to music about love, they think about love, they talk about it, and some of them fall in and out of it weekly. Adolescents pay attention to stories about love because they really want to know what it is and they want models for their behavior.

Protagonists in these films about love and romance range in age from twelve to eighteen, and the intensity of the attraction varies from film to film. All of the films do, however, share the following four essential attributes:

1. The characters try to figure out what real love is and how it differs from friendship, infatuation, and physical attraction.

2. The protagonists focus on finding the "right one" and then how to keep the romance alive. In some of the films a character has to choose between two possible partners. Sometimes several relationships are portrayed in a film and they contrast with the central relationship.

3. There is often a best friend or an adult in whom the main character confides.

4. There are stages in the relationship, and by the end of the movie the relationship works out or it doesn't, and the protagonists come to some realization about love.

Annotated List of Films

Information provided for each film is title, country (if other than the United States), director, year of release, MPAA rating, length, and language (if other than English). Films are in alphabetical order by title.

Angus (Patrick Read Johnson, 1995, PG-13, 87 min.)

For annotation see Chapter Eight.

Benny & Joon (Jeremiah S. Chechik, 1993, PG, 98 min.)

For annotation see Chapter Eight.

Cinema Paradiso (Italy, Giuseppe Tornatore, 1989, NR, 123 min., in Italian.)

For annotation see Chapter Six.

Clueless (Amy Heckerling, 1995, PG-13, 97 min.)

For annotation see Chapter Eight.

Elvira Madigan (Sweden, Bo Widerberg, 1967, PG, 89 min., in Swedish.)

In this international hit based on a true story, a nobleman elopes with a tightrope dancer to spend a romantic summer—at least until they run out of money.

Gregory's Girl (Scotland, Bill Forsyth, 1981, NR, 87 min.)

Gregory, a gawky teenager, plays soccer on his school team. When Dorothy joins the previously all-boy team, Gregory falls in love for the first time. Gregory is an appealing character whose vulnerability will strike a chord in younger teenagers.

Lucas (David Seltzer, 1986, PG-13, 100 min.)

For annotation see Chapter Eight.

The Man in the Moon (Robert Mulligan, 1991, PG-13, 99 min.)

Two sisters, one fourteen years old and one eighteen years old, fall in love with the same neighbor boy in the summer of 1957 in rural Louisiana. During this summer, they each learn about life, love, and death. This film shows a tightly knit family with a particularly strong and honest relationship between the younger sister and her father.

Mask (Peter Bogdanovich, 1985, PG-13, 120 min.)

For annotation see Chapter Eight.

My American Cousin (Canada, Sandy Wilson, 1985, PG, 94 min.)

Feisty twelve-year-old Sandy Wilcox complains that nothing ever happens on her ranch in Canada. All that changes when Butch, her college-age American cousin, arrives for a visit in his Cadillac convertible. While Sandy enjoys Butch's exploits, her parents are horrified by his influence on their daughter. The film explores the themes of growing up, taking responsibility, and family relationships.

My Brilliant Career (Australia, Gillian Armstrong, 1979, G, 102 min.)

For annotation see Chapter Six.

Rich in Love (Bruce Beresford, 1993, PG-13, 105 min.)

For annotation see Chapter Six.

A Room with a View (James Ivory, 1986, NR, 117 min.)

In this magnificent adaptation of E. M. Forster's novel of Victorian England, Lucy Honeychurch is simultaneously horrified and thrilled when George Emerson grabs and kisses her in a meadow outside Florence, Italy. Nevertheless, when she returns home to England, she accepts the marriage proposal of the very dull Cecil Vyse. The film follows Lucy's dilemma: Will she marry Cecil or will she finally acknowledge her own passionate side and accept George?

Running on Empty (Sidney Lumet, 1988, PG-13, 116 min.)

For annotation see Chapter Seven.

Sitting in Limbo (Canada, John N. Smith, 1986, PG, 95 min.)

For annotation see Chapter Six.

This Is My Life (Nora Ephron, 1992, PG, 94 min.)

For annotation see Chapter Six.

The Umbrellas of Cherbourg (France, Jacques Demy, 1964, NR, 90 min., in French.)

A teenage girl, daughter of a widow who owns an umbrella shop, falls in love with an auto mechanic, who is then drafted into the army. Shortly after he leaves for Algeria, she learns she is pregnant.

Told entirely in songs by Michel Legrand, this movie is romantic, joyous, sad, and poignant—with breathtaking color cinematography.

The Year My Voice Broke (Australia, John Duigan, 1987, PG-13, 103 min.)

Set in New South Wales in 1962, this film tells the story of Danny and Freya, best friends since they were children. Now that they are in high school, Danny wants Freya to be his girlfriend, but she has become the town's "wild girl" and is drawn to Trevor, a boy older and more experienced than Danny. Nevertheless, the two friends remain fiercely loyal to each other. Danny is a sometimes pitiful, but always appealing character; Freya is strong and willful, but tender-hearted, particularly in her attention to her ill grandmother.

The Essential Attributes of Films About Love and Romance

What Is Real Love?

Protagonists in films about love and romance are discovering love for the first time. Sometimes this discovery leaves them astounded and causes them to alter their behavior. Gregory (*Gregory's Girl*) seems to be totally at a loss as to how to behave when a girl joins his soccer team. Lucas (*Lucas*), a nerdy twelve-year-old, meets a new girl and—to everyone's astonishment—goes out for the football team to get her attention. These characters don't seem to realize that they are in love; they simply are obsessed with the attraction.

Sometimes, characters *know* that they are in love. Angus Bethune (*Angus*) has loved Melissa Lefevre since kindergarten, and spends weeks practicing so he will know how to dance with her at their school's Winter Ball. Cher (*Clueless*) has spent years bickering with her stepbrother Josh, but as the movie progresses, it becomes increasingly clear that Josh cares about Cher. The climax of the film is an "aha" moment when Cher realizes that she is in love with Josh. A similar moment occurs in *The Man in the Moon* when a younger sister realizes she is in love with her older sister's boyfriend.

Finding and Keeping the "Right One"

Protagonists in films about love and romance are often actively looking for romance. In *My American Cousin*, Sandy is looking for romance. So when her cousin shows up in his convertible, the attraction between the two is inevitable. Erica (*This is My Life*), on the other hand, is matter-of-fact and unromantic until she meets a young man and has her first experience with love.

Sometimes characters have to choose between two possible partners. Lucy (*A Room with a View*) is engaged to pedantic, steady Cecil Vyse, but she finds herself becoming attracted to the more impulsive and passionate George Emerson. Freya (*The Year My Voice Broke*) neglects her old friend Danny for the more experienced and exciting Trevor. Genevieve (*The Umbrellas of Cherbourg*) gives up the lover she adores to marry a man who will save her from the shame of being an unwed mother.

Occasionally romance films have other, secondary relationships that contrast with or support the central relationship. When Danny (*Running on Empty*) falls in love, his relationship is seen in the context of the loving relationship of his own parents. On the other hand, Freya (*The Year My Voice Broke*) is trying to establish a relationship with Trevor in the shadow of the bitter marriage of her mother and stepfather. *Clueless* contains several romances: Cher falls in love with her stepbrother Josh, her friend Dionne has a steady relationship, and their protegé falls in love several times.

Best Friends and Confidants

Teenagers in love want to share their experiences with someone. Sometimes the confidant is an adult. When Angus tells his grandfather about his love for Melissa and his fears of looking foolish at the Winter Ball, the grandfather arranges for dance lessons and rents a tuxedo for his nervous grandson. Salvatore (*Cinema Paradiso*) is deeply in love and he shows his love by following the girl around the streets of his Italian village taking movies of her. Alfredo, the projectionist at Cinema Paradiso, is Salvatore's confidant as he agonizes over his infatuation. Danny (*Running on Empty*), Rocky (*Mask*), and Genevieve (*Umbrellas of Cherbourg*) confide in their parents and receive support and good advice.

Sometimes the confidant is a peer. Freya (*The Year My Voice Broke*) shares her love for Trevor with her childhood friend Danny, making Danny miserable because he is—and always has been—totally in love with Freya. Cher (*Clueless*) confides both in her best friend Dionne and in her stepbrother Josh, and in us, the viewers.

Stages in the Relationship

Romances in these films typically develop by stages. The relationship often moves from that of mutual antagonism to friendship to attraction, as in *Clueless*, *The Man in the Moon*, and *A Room with a View*. Other films depict instant and almost total infatuation. Genevieve and Guy (*The Umbrellas of Cherbourg*) are hopelessly in love. They promise each other their love will last forever and they constantly write letters when they are separated. Elvira Madigan and her soldier are also totally infatuated with each other to the point where they cannot live apart.

These films about love and romance have either tragic, bittersweet, or happy endings. When it becomes clear that their relationship cannot work, Elvira Madigan and her nobleman lover kill themselves. Two sisters in *The Man in the Moon* fall in love with the same man, tearing their family apart. The two reconcile when their boyfriend dies tragically. *The Umbrellas of Cherbourg* has a bittersweet ending. Although Genevieve has pledged that she will wait forever for Guy to complete his tour of duty in the army, when she discovers she is pregnant, she agrees to a marriage arranged by her mother. At the end of the film the lovers meet briefly and part, acknowledging that they have gone their separate ways.

Occasionally in films about romance the protagonist is willing to end a relationship for a higher calling. Sybilla (*My Brilliant Career*) has the chance to marry a man with whom she would be very happy, but she chooses not to marry him—or anyone else—in order to have a career. Danny (*Running on Empty*) is clearly willing to sacrifice his relationship to stay with his family.

Other films have romances with happy endings. Lucy Honeychurch (*A Room with a View*) marries a man she loves and who adores her. In *Benny & Joon*, Joon falls in love with the eccentric Sam and makes plans to live with him. Pat and Fabian (*Sitting in Limbo*) work hard with their marriage and their responsibilities, but it obvious the two are happy with the choices they have made.

Writing Assignments

1. Choose one film from the list and write an essay analyzing how that film treats each of the four essential attributes of films about love and romance.

2. Compare a movie in which the central love affair works out (as in *Benny & Joon, Sitting in Limbo,* or *A Room with a View*) with a film with a love affair that does not work out (*Elvira Madigan, My Brilliant Career, The Man in the Moon,* or *Umbrellas of Cherbourg*). Analyze the relationships in each film to explain why one succeeds and the other fails.

3. Compare and contrast a comic romance film, like *Clueless* or *A Room with a View,* with a classic screwball comedy, like *The Philadelphia Story* or *Bringing Up Baby.*

4. (a) Analyze the cinematic elements of at least three romantic scenes from one or more films on the list. What do you notice about the cinematography, editing, and music in each scene? Write a paragraph describing the cinematography of each scene. (b) Write a shooting script or storyboard for a romantic scene from a romantic novel such as Francesca Lia Block's *Weetzie Bat,* Jenny Davis's *Sex Education,* or M. E. Kerr's *I Stay Near You.*

5. Except for Genevieve and Guy (*The Umbrellas of Cherbourg*), none of the characters in the films on the list write letters to each other. Choose a romantic film and write an exchange of love letters between the characters.

6. Choose a television show that has a plot driven by love. Then characterize the romance portrayed on the show. Write an essay comparing love on the television show with love in one of the films on the list.

Appendix A

Guidelines for Off-Air Recording of Broadcast Programming for Educational Purposes[1]

1. The guidelines were developed to apply only to off-air recording by nonprofit educational institutions.

2. A broadcast program may be recorded off-air simultaneously with broadcast transmission (including simultaneous cable retransmission) and retained by a nonprofit educational institution for a period not to exceed the first forty-five (45) consecutive calendar days after date of recording. Upon conclusion of such retention period, all off-air recordings must be erased or destroyed immediately. "Broadcast programs" are television programs transmitted by television stations for reception by the general public without charge.

3. Off-air recordings may be used once by individual teachers in the course of relevant teaching activities, and repeated once only when instructional reinforcement is necessary, in classrooms and similar places devoted to instruction within a single building, cluster, or campus, as well as in the homes of students receiving formalized home instruction, during the first ten (10) consecutive school days in the forty-five (45) day calendar day retention period. "School days" are school session days—not counting weekends, holidays, vacations, examination periods, and other sched-

uled interruptions—within the forty-five (45) calendar day retention period.

4. Off-air recordings may be made only at the request of and used by individual teachers, and may not be regularly recorded in anticipation of requests. No broadcast program may be recorded off-air more than once at the request of the same teacher, regardless of the number of times the program may be broadcast.

5. A limited number of copies may be reproduced from each off-air recording to meet the legitimate needs of teachers under these guidelines. Each such additional copy shall be subject to all provisions governing the original recording.

6. After the first ten (10) consecutive school days, off-air recordings may be used up to the end of the forty-five (45) calendar day retention period only for teacher evaluation purposes, i.e., to determine whether or not to include the broadcast program in the teaching curriculum, and may not be used in the recording institution for student exhibition or any other non-evaluation purposes without authorization.

7. Off-air recordings need not be used in their entirety, but the recorded programs may not be altered from their original content. Off-air recordings may not be physically or electronically combined or merged to constitute teaching anthologies or compilations.

8. All copies of off-air recording must include the copyright notice on the broadcast program as recorded.

9. Educational institutions are expected to establish appropriate control procedures to maintain the integrity of these guidelines.

Note

1. *Congressional Record.* October 14, 1981, p. E4751. Reprinted in Miller, J. K., et al. 1989. *Video Copyright Permissions: A Guide to Securing Permission to Retain, Perform, and Transmit Television Programs Videotaped Off the Air.* Friday Harbor, WA: Copyright Information Services, 25–26.

Appendix B

Recommended Young Adult Novels for Thematic Units

Coming of Age

Bridgers, S. E. 1979. *All Together Now*. New York: Bantam Books.

Brooks, B. 1984. *The Moves Make the Man*. New York: Harper & Row.

Crutcher, C. 1983. *Running Loose*. New York: Dell.

Davis, T. 1992. *If Rock and Roll Were a Machine*. New York: Delacorte Press.

Holland, I. 1972. *Man without a Face*. New York: Harper & Row.

Magorian, M. 1992. *Not a Swan*. New York: HarperCollins.

McCorkle, J. 1990. *Ferris Beach*. Chapel Hill: Algonquin Books.

Myers, W. D. 1988. *Fallen Angels*. New York: Scholastic Book Services.

Myers, W. D. 1988. *Scorpions*. New York: Harper & Row.

Nelson, T. 1989. *And One For All*. New York: Orchard Books.

Paulsen, G. 1987. *Hatchet*. New York: Puffin Books.

Paulsen, G. 1992. *The Haymeadow*. New York: Delacorte Press.

Thesman, J. 1991. *The Rain Catchers*. Boston: Houghton Mifflin.

Thompson, J. 1985. *Discontinued*. New York: Scholastic Book Services.

Voigt, C. 1982. *Dicey's Song*. New York: Atheneum.

Families

Armstrong, W. 1969. *Sounder*. New York: Harper & Row.

Bridgers, S. E. 1987. *Permanent Connections*. New York: HarperCollins.

Brooks, B. 1986. *Midnight Hour Encores*. New York: Harper & Row.

Cannon, A. E. 1991. *Amazing Gracie*. New York: Delacorte Press.

Carter, A. 1985. *Wart, Son of Toad*. New York: Berkley Books.

Crutcher, C. 1987. *Crazy Horse Electric Game*. New York: Dell.

Crutcher, C. 1989. *Chinese Handcuffs*. New York: Greenwillow Books.

Crutcher, C. 1995. *Ironman*. New York: Greenwillow Books.

Gibbons, K. 1987. *Ellen Foster*. Chapel Hill: Algonquin Books.

Hamilton, V. 1993. *Plain City*. New York: Scholastic Book Services.

Johnson, A. 1993. *Toning the Sweep*. New York: Scholastic Book Services.

Lynch, C. 1993. *Shadow Boxer*. New York: HarperCollins.

Lynch, C. 1994. *Iceman*. New York: HarperCollins.

Magorian, M. 1981. *Good Night, Mr. Tom*. New York: HarperCollins.

Mazer, N. F. 1987. *After the Rain*. New York: Avon.

Myers, W. D. 1992. *Somewhere in the Darkness*. New York: Scholastic Book Services.

Newton, S. 1986. *I Will Call It Georgie's Blues*. New York: Dell.

Paterson, K. 1980. *Jacob Have I Loved*. New York: Avon.

Peck, R. 1972. *A Day No Pigs Would Die*. New York: Dell.

Sweeney, J. 1995. *The Tiger Orchard*. New York: Dell.

Voigt, C. 1982. *Dicey's Song*. New York: Atheneum.

Weaver, W. 1993. *Striking Out*. New York: HarperCollins.

Belonging

Carter, A. 1989. *Up Country*. New York: Scholastic Book Services.

Childress, A. 1973. *A Hero Ain't Nothing But a Sandwich*. New York: Avon.

Cole, B. 1987. *The Goats*. New York: Farrar, Straus & Giroux.

Cormier, R. 1974. *The Chocolate War*. New York: Dell.

Crew, L. 1989. *Children of the River*. New York: Delacorte Press.

Crutcher, C. 1993. *Staying Fat for Sarah Byrnes*. New York: Greenwillow Books.

Garland, S. 1993. *Shadow of the Dragon*. San Diego: Harcourt Brace.

Hinton, S. E. 1967. *The Outsiders*. New York: Dell.

Hinton, S. E. 1975. *Rumblefish*. New York: Delacorte Press.

Hinton, S. E. 1988. *Taming the Star Runner*. New York: Dell.

Holman, F. 1974. *Slake's Limbo*. New York: Scribner.

Klass, D. 1994. *California Blue*. New York: Scholastic Book Services.

Lipsyte, R. 1977. *One Fat Summer*. New York: Bantam Books.

Peck, R. 1985. *Remembering the Good Times*. New York: Dell.

Philbrick, R. 1993. *Freak the Mighty*. New York: Scholastic Book Services.

Sleator, W. 1974. *House of Stairs*. New York: Dutton.

Voigt, C. 1983. *A Solitary Blue*. New York: Atheneum.

Williams-Garcia, R. 1995. *Like Sisters on the Homefront*. New York: Lodestar Books.

Dreams and Quests

Adams, R. 1974. *Watership Down*. New York: MacMillan.

Cormier, R. 1977. *I Am the Cheese*. New York: Dell.

Deuker, C. 1988. *On the Devil's Court*. Boston: Little, Brown.

George, J. 1969. *My Side of the Mountain*. New York: Dutton.

Hughes, M. 1990. *Invitation to the Game*. New York: Simon & Schuster.

LeGuin, U. K. 1968. *A Wizard of Earthsea*. New York: Parnassus.

Lipsyte, R. 1967. *The Contender*. New York: Bantam Books.

Lipsyte, R. 1991. *The Brave*. New York: HarperCollins.

Myers, W. D. 1981. *Hoops*. New York: Dell.

Lowry, L. 1993. *The Giver*. Boston: Houghton Mifflin.

Marino, J. 1992. *Like Some Kind of Hero*. Boston: Little, Brown.

Newton, S. 1986. *I Will Call It Georgie's Blues*. New York: Dell.

Paterson, K. 1975. *The Master Puppeteer*. New York: HarperCollins.

Pearce, P. 1992. *Tom's Midnight Garden*. New York: Harper Trophy.

Salinger, J. D. 1951. *The Catcher in the Rye*. Boston: Little, Brown.

Serraillier, I. 1963. *Escape from Warsaw*. New York: Scholastic Book Services.

Stone, B. 1985. *Half-Nelson, Full-Nelson*. New York: Harper & Row.

Thompson, J. 1986. *Band of Angels*. New York: Scholastic Book Services.

Tolkien, J. R. R. 1966. *The Hobbit, or, There and Back Again*. Boston: Houghton Mifflin.

Wolff, V. E. 1993. *Make Lemonade*. New York: Scholastic Book Services.

Zindel, P. 1985. *Harry and Hortense at Hormone High*. New York: Bantam Books.

Love and Romance

Bauer, J. 1992. *Squashed*. New York: Delacorte Press.

Bauer, J. 1995. *Thwonk*. New York: Dell.

Block, F. L. 1989. *Weetzie Bat*. New York: HarperCollins.

Byars, B. 1989. *Bingo Brown and the Language of Love*. New York: Viking Kestrel.

Cather, W. 1961. *My Antonía*. Boston: Houghton Mifflin.

Conford, E. 1983. *If This Is Love, I'll Take Spaghetti*. New York: Scholastic Book Services.

Daly, M. 1942. *Seventeenth Summer*. New York: Dodd, Mead.

Daly, M. 1986. *Acts of Love*. New York: Scholastic Book Services.

Davis, J. 1988. *Sex Education*. New York: Dell.

Foley, J. 1991. *Susanna Siegelbaum Gives Up Guys*. New York: Scholastic Book Services.

Greene, B. 1973. *Summer of My German Soldier*. New York: Dial Press.

Greene, C. 1986. *The Love Letters of J. Timothy Owens*. New York: Harper & Row.

Kerr, M. E. 1985. *I Stay Near You*. New York: Berkley Books.

Koertge, R. 1986. *Where the Kissing Never Stops*. New York: Avon.

Koertge, R. 1988. *The Arizona Kid*. New York: Avon.

McKinley, R. 1978. *Beauty: A Retelling of Beauty and the Beast*. New York: Harper.

Myers, W. D. 1987. *Motown and Didi: A Love Story*. New York: NAL-Dutton.

Namioka, L. 1994. *April and the Dragon Lady*. San Diego: Harcourt Brace.

Tamar, E. 1994. *The Things I Did Last Summer*. San Diego: Harcourt Brace.

Appendix C

Recommended Periodicals to Support Film Study

We've found the following periodicals helpful—as background reading for us, as sources for film reviews, and as secondary sources for students' independent study. Some of these are available at newsstands, others are available by subscription only. All of them would be appropriate for high school media centers. (If a periodical has more than one address, we have included the subscription address rather than that of the editorial office.)

American Cinematographer. Monthly journal of the American Society of Cinematographers. Published by ASC Holding Corp., PO Box 2230, Hollywood, CA 90078 (800-448-0145).

Cinefantastique. Monthly magazine about horror, fantasy, and science fiction films. PO Box 270, Oak Park, IL 60303 (800-798-6515).

Film Comment. Bimonthly journal of the Film Society of Lincoln Center, 70 Lincoln Center Plaza, New York, NY 10023-6595 (800-783-4903).

MovieMaker. Articles about and interviews with filmmakers. Describes itself as a magazine "for the audience and the artist." Published by Rice Entertainment, 301 Belmont Avenue East, Seattle, WA 98102 (206-860-3831).

Premiere. PO Box 55389, Boulder, CO 80323-5389. *Premiere* is the most accessible yet comprehensive film magazine for the general public. Regular features include news of upcoming films, interviews with filmmakers and actors, "shot-by-shot" descriptions of key scenes from popular films, and the ruminations of the inimitable Libby Gelman-Waxner.

Scenario: The Magazine of Screenwriting Art. Contains four complete screenplays in each issue as well as articles and interviews with screenwriters. Published quarterly by RC Publications, Inc., 3200 Tower Oaks Boulevard, Rockville, MD 20852 (800-222-2654).

scr(i)pt. Focuses on screenwriting. Published bimonthly by Forum, Inc., 5638 Sweet Air Road, Baldwin, MD 21013-9009 (410-592-3466).